explore

the Southeast
National Marine Sanctuaries

WITH JEAN-MICHEL COUSTEAU

explore

the Southeast National Marine Sanctuaries

WITH JEAN-MICHEL COUSTEAU

FLORIDA KEYS | GRAY'S REEF | FLOWER GARDEN BANKS

OCEAN PUBLISHING

Copyright © 2011 by Ocean Futures Society

ISBN 978-0-9826940-1-5

Book cover, layout and design by Nate Myers, Wilhelm Design
Maps by Gary Rosenberg

Printed in the United States of America

Front Cover: Ocean Futures Team Member Holly Lohuis with hawksbill turtle.
Photo credit: Carrie Vonderhaar, Ocean Futures Society.

10 9 8 7 6 5 4 3 2 1

Library of Congress Cataloging-in-Publication Data

Explore the Southeast national marine sanctuaries with Jean-Michel Cousteau / Ocean Futures Society.
    p. cm.
ISBN 978-0-9826940-1-5 (alk. paper)
 1. Marine parks and reserves--Southern States--Guidebooks. 2. United States. National Ocean Service. Office of National Marine Sanctuaries--Guidebooks. 3. Southern States--Guidebooks. I. Cousteau, Jean-Michel. II. Ocean Futures Society.
QH91.75.U6E8 2011
578.770973--dc22

                    2010046101

Praise for

Explore the National Marine Sanctuaries with Jean-Michel Cousteau

"This book series gives us deeply felt and profound insight into our country's amazing National Marine Sanctuaries. They are wonderful, illuminating volumes that show the sanctuaries' great beauty and awe. In this critical time of a major oil disaster threatening our natural world, there is an urgent need for the world to learn about these momentous marine sanctuaries and how to protect them. I thank my dear friend, Jean-Michel Cousteau, and Ocean Futures Society, for calling attention to the care of these beautiful marine sanctuaries in our time of extreme need. Jean-Michel is the authoritative servant on the sea for our generation and future generations. This incredible series will be beneficial in getting the word out about the importance of protecting our oceans and the marine life that call it home."

Robert Lyn Nelson
Artist/Environmentalist

"Jean-Michel Cousteau and Ocean Futures Society have set themselves the task of communicating the beauty of the ocean and the necessity of protecting it to the widest possible audience. Through stunning photography and superbly succinct writing, Explore the National Marine Sanctuaries with Jean-Michel Cousteau *does just that. This wonderful book series shows how very precious the*

USA's National Marine Sanctuaries are, and what a huge contribution the sanctuaries make to our knowledge and understanding of the underwater world. The series is also very timely in light of recent events in the Gulf of Mexico which show how vulnerable the marine environment still is. Oil spillages do not respect marine sanctuaries any more than forest fires respect the boundaries of National Parks.

But without even the protection that the National Marine Sanctuaries offer, America's marine biodiversity—and the public knowledge and appreciation of it—would be the poorer. Those of us whose lives revolve around the protection of wildlife on land, rather than the marine environment, can only admire and envy Jean-Michel's extraordinary success in conserving, communicating and educating. Genuine environmentalists like Jean-Michel know that we need a truly holistic approach to the conservation of wildlife on land and sea. This book series is an undoubted 'treasure-house' and I have no hesitation in recommending it to all who love wildlife and wish to understand better how to redress the terrible imbalance between Man and Nature."

Simon Cowell MBE FRGS MCIJ
Founder, Wildlife Aid; Producer and
Presenter, Wildlife SOS, United Kingdom

"Marine sanctuaries represent the most special places in the ocean. We cannot sustain the ocean without first sustaining our sanctuaries. But like all things in the ocean, they are beneath the surface and invisible to almost everyone. Jean-Michel, through his films and this book series, gives these life and makes the ocean visible and tangible. He is a keen observer of nature and a storyteller about the ocean. He adds a depth of understanding and interpretation that is easy for everyone to grasp."

Daniel J. Basta, Director
NOAA's Office of National Marine Sanctuaries

"Jean-Michel Cousteau and his team have put together an amazing series of books dedicated to the undersea world on which we depend. This is the first time anyone has truly captured the experience of diving America's underwater treasures, the entire national marine sanctuary system. I cannot tell you how truly beautiful and moving a series this is. After spending time with this book, I am even more proud of America's commitment to protect our National Marine Sanctuaries."

Jeff Mora, Los Angeles Lakers executive chef,
board member National Marine Sanctuary Foundation,
International Advisory Board member Ocean Futures Society

"National Marine Sanctuaries are not only extraordinary places to visit, they are also one of our most powerful tools in ocean conservation. Explore the National Marine Sanctuaries with Jean-Michel Cousteau *provides an underwater roadmap through the Sanctuaries with compelling stories and magnificent images. For those fortunate enough to have visited Sanctuaries, these books are the perfect way to preserve the memories. For those who have not, they are the next best thing to being there. Most importantly,* Explore the National Marine Sanctuaries with Jean-Michel Cousteau *teaches us that by protecting National Marine Sanctuaries we help protect the world-ocean...and ourselves."*

Bob Talbot Chairman of the Board,
National Marine Sanctuary Foundation;
Board of Directors, Sea Shepherd Conservation Society,
Filmmaker and Photographer

Contents

Foreword

Jean-Michel Cousteau's love of the ocean and the desire to protect it began as a boy, inspired by living on the edge of the Mediterranean Sea and sharing underwater adventures in the Atlantic, Pacific and Indian oceans with his parents, brother, and other pioneering ocean explorers aboard the legendary ship, *Calypso*. Ask him what it is about the ocean that has captured his heart and mind, and he might tell you of face-to-face encounters with curious fish, squid and great white sharks or the joy of gliding through forests of kelp or being underwater at night surrounded by a living cosmos of bioluminescent creatures. He could say how rewarding it is to be an explorer, to be the first to see places and meet forms of life in the sea that have not yet been given names. And, he would likely encourage you to go experience such things for yourself in places such as those celebrated in this volume and others that follow.

Cousteau's deep commitment to the National Marine Sanctuary Program stems from understanding how important the sanctuaries are as a means of protecting the nation's natural, historic and cultural heritage. Like national parks and wildlife management areas on the land, marine sanctuaries safeguard healthy systems and help restore those that have been harmed. While some observers believe the ocean should be able to take care of itself, many species prized for food or sport have declined by 90 percent or more in a few decades. Low oxygen areas, "dead zones," are proliferating, and sea grass meadows and coral reefs are diminishing. Major changes, most not favorable to humankind, are underway, and the sanctuaries can give stressed systems and species a break. We need the oceans, and now the oceans need us to do what it takes to restore health to the world's blue heart.

I share with Jean-Michel Cousteau the delight of being sprayed with whale breath at Stellwagen Bank, dodging sea turtles while looking for fossils of ice age animals at Gray's Reef off the coast of Georgia, of gliding among giant parrotfish in the Florida Keys, and immersing myself in a blizzard of eggs from spawning coral at the Flower Garden Banks off the coasts of Texas and Louisiana. There is haunting beauty and mystery in the protected shipwrecks lying within the Great Lakes, and others such as the remains of the Civil War vessel, *Monitor*, once a home for sailors, now a sanctuary for clouds of small fish and large grouper.

Those who visit any of California's four National Marine Sanctuaries have a chance to glimpse blue whales, the largest animals on earth, as well as some of the smallest, the minute planktonic creatures that drive ocean food webs. The Olympic National Marine Sanctuary holds healthy kelp forests adjacent to stands of ancient trees, and westward, in the Hawaiian Islands, special protection is being provided for some notable annual visitors, humpback whales. Coral reefs and the enormous diversity of life they contain are valued – and protected – in the Northwest Hawaiian Islands, American Samoa and a series of reefs, atolls and deep canyons near the Mariana Islands. These are all vital parts of the nation's treasury, places that give hope for the ocean, and therefore hope for ourselves.

I am pleased to be associated with the Ocean Futures Society, the organization Jean-Michel Cousteau founded to explore, communicate discoveries and messages to people and inspire them to take action to restore and protect the living ocean. They are making a difference – and so can you. Your reading of this book series is a strong first step in your understanding of the importance of protecting the sanctuaries for generations to come.

Dr. Sylvia Earle
Oakland, California

Preface

The National Marine Sanctuary sites were designated in part because they were imperiled. Created more than 100 years after the national park system, these underwater treasures have been more difficult to explore and we have worked hard to learn their true value. By the time we did, we also discovered they were already at risk. Their very existence speaks to a reality that we now understand. It is clear they protect and promote the abundance and diversity of marine life essential to a healthy ocean. I am gratified that our leaders have seen the wisdom of placing a priority on protecting them now and for the future.

So it is ironic that this first book in the series on America's Underwater treasures is going to press at a perilous time. The largest oil spill in the history of the United States has recently taken place with the Deepwater Horizon spill contaminating the Gulf of Mexico with unpredictable impacts on the one sanctuary located there; but because of the Loop Current and the Gulf Stream, all the Sanctuaries of the Southeast region are potentially at some risk. The environmental consequences of the oil spill to the Gulf and the entire Atlantic seashore will take years to understand. A massive cleanup effort is in force with no end in sight.

It is an incident of almost mythological proportions. We have opened the Pandora's Box of what we thought was the cheap energy of petroleum. We are finding it is costing us too many lives, too much environmental degradation, and far too much impact on climate change. But how can we go back on the luxuries cheap oil has provided? How willing are we to protect the natural world on which we ultimately depend? The story of this spill will be studied for decades and passed on in personal family histories for generations. It is a turning point. But in which direction will we turn?

It may take longer than we would like, but I am confident the Gulf of Mexico will somewhat recover and that ultimately we will move away from petroleum to safe, clean, inventive, renewable, alternative sources. We will look to innovations that don't pollute the air or the water and that don't carry the risks of oil drilling or nuclear power. We may use nuclear power but in units small enough to light only a city block and never so big as to condemn all surrounding life in perpetuity in case of an accident. And petroleum will eventually be depleted or too expensive to extract and be phased out.

We may harness the sun, the wind, the waves, deep undersea currents, the energy in chemical reactions, or that generated from differences in temperature from cold, deep water pumped to the warm surface. We haven't even begun to imagine what may be ahead that is exponentially better because we have been drugged by what exists. But we no longer will accept the high price to the environment and to human life so blatantly visible by this horrific oil spill.

The Gulf of Mexico will recover and its Sanctuaries will continue as emblems of how we proceed with our precious natural resources everywhere. The concept of Marine Protected Areas and Sanctuaries will expand and will re-seed and enliven vast areas of our imperiled sea.

For now, enjoy the splendors in this book, realize what has been at risk, demand better than we now have, and then do everything you can to make it happen at every level.

This book shows you what is at stake.

Jean-Michel Cousteau
Santa Barbara, California

Introduction

About this Series

The four-book series, *Explore the National Marine Sanctuaries with Jean-Michel Cousteau,* has been developed in partnership with the National Marine Sanctuary system and Ocean Futures Society. Text in *italics* is excerpted from the previously-published (2007), limited-edition book *America's Underwater Treasures* by Jean-Michel Cousteau and Julie Robinson with photography by Carrie Vonderhaar. That book describes the experience and research of Jean-Michel and his Ocean Futures Team while diving all 13 underwater marine sanctuaries and the one underwater marine monument. Their experiences are captured in an award-winning film by the same name aired on PBS as part of *Jean-Michel Cousteau's Ocean Adventures.* This series is offered to make information on these vital sanctuaries even more inclusive for the American public.

Each book in the series takes readers to one of the four regions of the country into which NOAA has organized its management of the National Marine Sanctuaries. This book, *Explore the Southeast National Marine Sanctuaries with Jean-Michel Cousteau,* visits sanctuaries in the Florida Keys, off coastal Georgia, and in the Gulf of Mexico off Texas and Louisiana. The other books in the series are: *Explore the West Coast National Marine Sanctuaries with Jean-Michel Cousteau; Explore the Northeast National Marine Sanctuaries with Jean-Michel*

Cousteau; and, *Explore the Pacific Islands National Marine Sanctuaries with Jean-Michel Cousteau.* All books are available individually or as a four-volume set.

Jean-Michel Cousteau.
Photo credit: Matthew Ferraro, Ocean Futures Society.

The first National Marine Sanctuary in the United States was established only three decades ago, while Yellowstone, the oldest of America's National Parks, was created in 1872. By comparison to parks, these natural marine jewels were damaged upon arrival. Only small portions remain pristine. For many, their designations arose amidst threats to one or a number of aspects to their survival. Like terrestrial parks, these are special habitats, managed zones for the recovery of critical species like humpback whales or juvenile rockfish but, most importantly, they attempt to preserve the integrity of the web of life.

Ironically, we discovered that managing these resources for sustainability was in truth an exercise in managing ourselves. And that's not, as we're still learning, an easy job. At each destination we were privileged witnesses to the real-time drama of marine conservation playing out across the United States. At the heart of it all, we found a powerful paradigm shift happening in environmentalism. Fishermen, environmentalists and scientists from opposite sides of the aisle were sitting down together with rolled-up sleeves, poring through scientific research, debating the merits of reserves and restoration, and coming to terms with this new definition of sanctuary. "These are," as Dan Basta, Director of the National Marine Sanctuary System, reminded us, "still works in progress."

About National Marine Sanctuaries

The Office of National Marine Sanctuaries, part of the National Oceanic and Atmospheric Administration (NOAA), manages a national system of underwater-protected areas. The National Marine Sanctuary Act (created in 1972) authorizes the Secretary of Commerce to designate specific areas as National Marine Sanctuaries to promote comprehensive management of their special ecological, historical, recreational, and aesthetic resources. There are currently thirteen National Marine Sanctuaries and one Marine National Monument managed by NOAA in areas where the natural or cultural resources are so significant that they warrant special status and protection.

On January 6, 2009, President George W. Bush established three additional marine national monuments, which were placed into the Pacific Reefs National Wildlife Refuge Complex. The three new marine national monuments are the Pacific Remote Islands Marine National Monument, Marianas Trench Marine National Monument, and the Rose Atoll Marine National Monument. Because Jean-Michel Cousteau and his Ocean Futures Society team have not yet dived in these three remote areas, they are not included in this series. Further, these new monuments are managed by the US Fish & Wildlife Service and not the National Oceanic & Atmospheric Administration, the managing agency of the national marine sanctuaries and one marine monument featured here.

The Office of National Marine Sanctuaries works cooperatively with the public and federal, state, and local officials to promote conservation while allowing compatible commercial and recreational activities in the Sanctuaries. Increasing public awareness of our marine heritage, scientific research, monitoring, exploration, educational programs, and outreach are just a few of the ways the Office of National Marine Sanctuaries fulfills its mission to the American people. The primary objective of a sanctuary is to protect its natural and cultural features while allowing people to use and enjoy the ocean in a sustainable way. Sanctuary waters provide a secure habitat for species close to extinction and protect historically significant shipwrecks and artifacts. Sanctuaries serve as natural classrooms and laboratories for schoolchildren and researchers alike to promote understanding and stewardship of our oceans. They often are cherished recreational spots for sport fishing and diving and support commercial industries such as tourism, fishing and kelp harvesting.

Today (2007), only 0.01 percent of the world's oceans are effectively protected, a comparatively small measure, and one most scientists are quick to caution isn't a panacea for all the ocean's troubles. But it's enough nonetheless, to keep some fisheries managers and fishermen hopeful about sustainably harvesting fish from the sea. In the face of collapsing fisheries, "They may help some exploited species recover and keep others from going entirely extinct," according to Daniel Pauly, a researcher with the Fisheries Center at the University of British Columbia. He postulates that marine protected areas "should help prevent this, just like forests and other natural terrestrial habitats have enabled the survival of wildlife species, which agriculture would have otherwise rendered extinct."

The mission of NOAA's National Marine Sanctuaries is to serve as the trustee for the nation's system of marine protected areas, to conserve, protect, and enhance their biodiversity, ecological integrity and cultural legacy. The National Marine Sanctuary System consists of fourteen protected areas that encompass more than 150,000 square miles of marine and Great Lakes waters from Washington State to the Florida Keys; from Lake Huron to American Samoa. The system includes thirteen national marine sanctuaries and the Northwestern Hawaiian Islands Marine National Monument. These sanctuaries embrace part of our collective riches as a nation. Within their protected waters, giant humpback whales breed and calve their young, temperate reefs flourish, and shipwrecks tell stories of our maritime history. Today, our marine sanctuary system encompasses deep ocean gardens, nearshore coral reefs, whale migration corridors, deep sea canyons, and even underwater archeological sites. The sites range in size from one-quarter square mile in Fagatele Bay, American Samoa, to more than 135,000 square miles in the Northwestern Hawaiian Islands, one of the largest marine protected areas in the world. Each sanctuary site is a unique place needing special protections. Natural classrooms, cherished recreational spots, and valuable commercial industries—marine sanctuaries represent many things to many people.

The National Marine Sanctuaries' Southeast Region

A healthy reef ecosystem is key to a healthy marine environment, and the office of the National Marine Sanctuary Southeast region includes three distinctive yet interconnected reef systems. The Florida Keys are major international tourist attractions known for abundant fishing, numerous coral reefs, and historic underwater archaeological sites. The **Florida Keys National Marine Sanctuary** is tasked with preserving these cultural and natural resources while allowing an increasing population of residents and visitors to access them. Seventeen miles off Georgia is **Gray's Reef National Marine Sanctuary**, which has one of the largest nearshore sandstone reefs in the southeastern United States. The northernmost coral reefs in the continental United States are located in the **Flower Gardens Banks National Marine Sanctuary**. The Flower Gardens coral reef community probably began developing on top of salt domes 10,000 to 15,000 years ago. The community has thrived sufficiently to obscure all trace of the deformed bedrock on which it developed, replacing it with dense coral reefs.

Florida Keys National Marine Sanctuary

"When I arrived at the Dry Tortugas and saw the goliath groupers, it reminded me of my youth in the Mediterranean Sea before large fish, and especially local groupers, were wiped out. It gave me hope because I realized that if we give them protected areas, they will come back, very well and very fast."
     —Jean-Michel Cousteau

Goliath grouper. Photo credit: Carrie Vonderhaar, Ocean Futures Society.

"It's my hope people will see that each individual can help the environmental situation, can help decrease pollution, help with water issues. Hopefully this will bring that message across, that each one of us as an individual is empowered to do something in our own way, whether it's shutting the water off when you brush your teeth, recycling in your hometown, working on a community project to protect land, or trying to create a park. All of those things make a difference."
     —Céline Cousteau

About the Florida Keys National Marine Sanctuary

Few marine environments in the U.S. compare to the Florida Keys in terms of natural beauty and natural resources. The Keys are located on the southern tip of the Florida peninsula, beginning just south of Key Biscayne and ending just 90 miles north of Cuba.

Aerial view of reefs and some of the smallest Florida Keys. Photo credit: Carrie Vonderhaar, Ocean Futures Society.

North America's only living coral barrier reef, and the third longest barrier reef in the world (following Australia and Belize), lies about six miles seaward of the Florida Keys (a 126-mile long string of islands extending south and west of the Florida mainland). Coral reefs contain more varieties of life than any other marine environment. They are part of a fragile interdependent ecosystem that includes mangroves and seagrasses that grow both on the ocean and bay side of the Florida Keys. In recognition of this important environment, the Florida Keys National Marine Sanctuary was created in 1990. In 2001, waters surrounding the Dry Tortugas were afforded full protection as an Ecological Reserve and included in the Florida Keys National Marine Sanctuary. The Tortugas Ecological Reserve is the largest marine reserve contiguous to North America.

The Sanctuary consists of 2,800 square nautical miles (9,500 square kilometers) of coastal and oceanic waters, and the submerged lands thereunder. It surrounds the Florida Keys, extending 220 miles from the tip of the Florida peninsula, stretching south, then westward to encompass the Tortugas islands, but excludes the Dry Tortugas National Park. The shoreward boundary of the Sanctuary is the mean high-water mark. Within these waters are spectacular, unique, and nationally significant marine environments, including seagrass meadows, mangrove islands, and extensive coral reefs. These marine environments support rich biological communities possessing extensive conservation, recreational, commercial, ecological, historical, research, educational, and aesthetic values that give this area special national significance. These environments are the marine equivalent of tropical rain forests in that they support high levels of biological diversity, are fragile and easily susceptible to damage from human activities, and possess high value if properly conserved.

US1 is the only road connecting most of the islands in the Florida Keys. Photo credit: Carrie Vonderhaar, Ocean Futures Society.

Soft corals like sea rods and sea fans are abundant on some reefs in the Florida Keys. Photo credit: Bill Precht, Florida Keys National Marine Sanctuary.

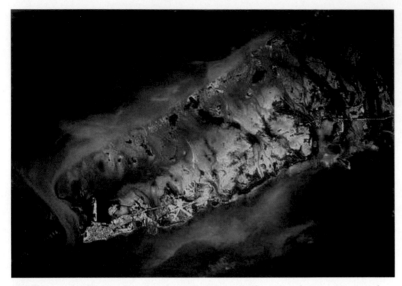

Satellite map of the lower Florida Keys. Photo credit: Florida Keys National Marine Sanctuary.

Conservation and restoration efforts in South Florida have been hampered by finger-pointing and deep-seated conflicts. But the Tortugas Reserve may be a beacon of hope in the fog of uncertainty and layers of doubt that have obscured much-needed action. As one of 23 no-take zones situated inside the boundaries of the Florida Keys National Marine Sanctuary, its unique location far from the impacts of human development serves as a reference site for how an intact reef ecosystem functions and how it looks. The protected Tortugas may also be a wellspring of life that eventually spills over and populates adjacent depleted habitats. Not all marine protected areas (MPAs) incorporate no-take zones, sometimes called marine reserves, by default. But those like the Tortugas are a new and evolving conservation management design. While as little as one percent of the Florida Keys National Marine Sanctuary is designated as no-take, tremendous gains were found within the first few years of establishment. Monitoring provided verification of the intuitive planning behind the reserve's design. Harvest-size spiny lobsters, groupers and snappers, were found in greater numbers and size inside the reserves, compared with non-protected sites. An analysis of MPAs around the world by the National Center for Ecological Analysis and Synthesis, found some very good news: "Population densities were on average 91 percent higher, biomass was 192 percent higher, average organism size was 31 percent higher, and species diversity was 23 percent higher," inside monitored marine reserve sites. The success of no-take zones, however, is heavily dependent upon careful consideration of location and size. Ocean circulation patterns and enforcement to protect spawning populations *and to maximize the export of larval and juvenile fish and invertebrates into adjacent waters are important considerations.*

Cultural resources are also contained within the sanctuary. The proximity of coral reefs to centuries old shipping routes has resulted in a high concentration of shipwrecks and an abundance of artifacts.

Carysfort Reef Lighthouse is located 5 miles off of Key Largo at Carysfort Reef. Since its completion in 1852, the lighthouse has served to warn vessels of the shallow reef. Photo credit: Florida Keys National Marine Sanctuary.

This complex marine ecosystem also supports tourism and commercial fishing, the economic foundation of the Florida Keys. In the last 20 years the tourism industry has grown considerably—visitors drive, fly or cruise each year to the most accessible tropical paradise in the Caribbean Basin. Tourists and semi-permanent residents increase the resident population of the Keys by 75 percent during "season" (November to April). This ecosystem's extensive nursery, feeding and breeding grounds also support a multi-million dollar commercial fishing industry.

Why a National Marine Sanctuary?

Warning signs that the Keys' environment and natural resources were fragile, and not infinite, came as early as the 1950s. Public outcry has cited pollution, overharvest, physical impacts, overuse, and use conflicts as continuing to occur in the Keys. These concerns continued to be voiced by environmentalists and scientists alike throughout the decade of the 1970s and into the 1990s.

Looe Key Mooring Buoy field. Photo credit: Florida Keys National Marine Sanctuary.

The deterioration of the marine environment in the Florida Keys has continued. There is a decline of healthy corals, signaled by an increase of coral diseases, coral bleaching, and decreased living coral cover. Marine scientists have reported an invasion of algae in seagrass beds and onto reefs. Fisheries scientists are reporting declines in some fish stocks and Florida Bay has undergone changes during the past decade that have resulted in degradation of the ecosystem's productivity, health, and stability. Factors such as reduced freshwater flow into Florida Bay have resulted in plankton blooms, sponge and seagrass die-offs, and fish kills.

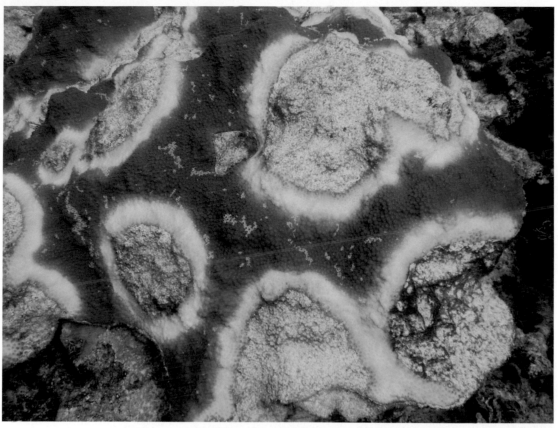

Diseased star coral. Photo credit: Diego Lirman. University of Miami.

In 1989, mounting threats to the health and ecological future of the coral reef ecosystem in the Florida Keys prompted Congress to take action to protect this fragile natural resource. The threat of oil drilling in the mid-1980s off the Florida Keys, combined with reports of deteriorating water quality throughout the region, occurred at the same time scientists were assessing the adverse effects of coral bleaching, the die-off of the long-spined sea urchin, loss of living coral cover on reefs, a major seagrass die-off, declines in reef fish populations, and the spread of coral disease. These were topics of major scientific concern, and the focus of several scientific workshops, when three large ships ran aground on the coral reef tract within 18 days in the fall of 1989. Coincidental as it may seem, it was this final physical insult to the reef that prompted Congress to take action to protect the coral reef ecosystem of the Florida Keys.

Long-spined sea urchin. Photo credit: Richard Murphy, Ocean Futures Society.

Just before midnight on August 10, 1994, the 155 foot research vessel, the R/V Columbus Iselin, owned and operated by the University of Miami, went aground on a spur and groove coral reef formation in the western portion of the Looe Key National Marine Sanctuary, now part of the Florida Keys National Marine Sanctuary. Photo credit: Florida Keys National Marine Sanctuary.

Although most remember the ship groundings as having triggered Congressional action, it was in fact the cumulative events of environmental degradation, in conjunction with the physical impacts, that prompted the designation of the 2800 square nautical mile Florida Keys National Marine Sanctuary on November 16, 1990 (incorporating Key Largo and Looe Key National Marine Sanctuaries.) This designation also called for the development of a comprehensive management plan for the region. In 2001, the Tortugas Ecological Reserve was established as part of the Florida Keys National Marine Sanctuary.

THE EVOLUTION OF THE FLORIDA KEYS NATIONAL MARINE SANCTUARY

- December, 1975: The Key Largo National Marine Sanctuary was designated (The US's second National Marine Sanctuary)
- January 1981: The Looe Key National Marine Sanctuary was designated
- November 1990: The Florida Keys National Marine Sanctuary was designated Key Largo and Looe Key Sanctuaries were incorporated into FKNMS
- 2001: Tortugas Ecological Reserve was established within FKNMS

Fort Jefferson in Dry Tortugas National Park. Photo credit: Carrie Vonderhaar, Ocean Futures Society.

From the ocean's surface and the glaring heat of the summer's last dog days, a shimmering mirage-like effect creates the illusion of the Tortugas being actually submerged. It's a phenomenon that has led unlucky mariners from Spanish sailors, to shrimp fishermen and drug runners, to lay claim to them from a watery grave. Viewed from a seaplane, the islands appear as a wasteland of littered wrecks, the skeletons of vessels lie like bleached bones marooned in a turquoise sea. The Tortugas are a chain of seven flat islands and adjacent reefs stretching from the southern tip of the Keys nearly to Cuba. The adjective "Dry" was added to Ponce de Leon's 1513 description of the Tortugas to mark their lack of fresh water on nautical charts. For centuries, they've been considered a no-man's land, brimming with hazards both natural and manmade. That is, until the late 1980s, when they captured the attention of a handful of marine scientists who found something surprisingly different about the Tortugas reefs: their vibrant health.

A calm summer's day in the Florida Keys National Marine Sanctuary. Photo credit: Carrie Vonderhaar, Ocean Futures Society.

This discovery of nearly pristine reefs so close to Florida's mainland spurred a conservation initiative, groundbreaking both in its scope and for the cross-section of support it eventually received. In 2001, waters surrounding the Dry Tortugas were afforded full protection as an Ecological Reserve and included in the Florida Keys National Marine Sanctuary. The Tortugas Ecological Reserve is the largest marine reserve contiguous to North America. Fishing is now prohibited and anchoring restricted. But a large section, the North Reserve, is open for divers to explore and the sanctuary has established moorings buoys for vessels.

Jean-Michel Cousteau dives beneath a sponge-covered ledge. Photo credit: Manuel Lazcano, Ocean Futures Society.

Resources within the Sanctuary

CORAL REEFS

Aerial view of coral reefs in the Florida Keys. Photo credit: Amy Massey, Florida Keys National Marine Sanctuary.

Coral reefs are generally classified into three types: barrier reefs, fringing reefs, and atolls. Barrier reefs and atolls are both characterized by a lagoon that is protected on the seaward side by the reef. Barrier reefs occur in association with continental land masses, whereas atolls are coral reefs that form atop submarine volcanoes. Fringing reefs are considered immature because they have not yet formed a lagoon in the backreef. Under less than ideal conditions, coral also exists in small communities or patch reefs.

Many varieties of corals can be found in the Florida Keys.
Photo credit: Florida Keys National Marine Sanctuary.

Angelfish swim amid sea whips.
Photo credit: Mike White, Florida Keys National Marine Sanctuary.

Colonies of tiny anemone-like polyps make up the living coral tissue. Within the tissue of most reef-building corals live small organisms that are capable of photosynthesizing or changing light energy into food. These organisms are called zooxanthellae, pronounced

"zo-zan-thel-ee." Although corals are carnivorous and feed on zooplankton, they receive much of their energy and oxygen as byproducts of zooxanthellae photosynthesis. The zooxanthellae also promote the rate of calcium carbonate production by the coral colony, thus, promoting growth. The relationship between coral colonies and zooxanthellae is called symbiosis. Symbiotic relationships are common among organisms living on coral reefs.

Close-up of star coral polyps.
Photo credit: Florida Keys National Marine Sanctuary.

Reef-building corals grow in size by increasing the amount of carbonate calcium in their skeleton and adding new living tissue to cover the larger skeleton. Under ideal conditions, some species of coral grow as boulders, which can be taller than an adult human. This process takes decades as boulder-type corals grow less than one centimeter per year. Thinner, branching corals grow as quickly as ten centimeters per year, but are easily broken in strong storms or as a result of human impact. The age of corals can be determined by examining coral

Pillar coral. Photo credit: Florida Keys National Marine Sanctuary.

growth rings, similar to counting rings in the trunk of a tree, or through the use of radioisotopes.

The rigidity of coral reefs helps protect the shoreline from destructive tropical storm waves. Reefs provide habitats for hundreds of species of marine organisms including commercially important finfish and shellfish. Ecologically speaking, coral reefs are diverse places, containing 22 of the 23 animal phyla found on the planet. Symbiotic relationships are common and add to the complexity of species interactions. Coral reefs are among the most productive habitats, and the oldest (400 million years) on earth.

Soft corals and sponges add color to the reefscape.
Photo credit: Florida Keys National Marine Sanctuary.

SEAGRASSES

Seagrasses are flowering plants that live underwater. Like land plants, seagrasses produce oxygen. The depth at which seagrasses are found is limited by water clarity—this determines the amount of light reaching the plant. Florida's estimated 2.7 million acres of seagrass meadows are important natural resources that perform many significant functions including:

- maintaining water clarity by trapping fine sediments and other particles in their leaves and roots;

- stabilizing the bottom with their roots and rhizomes in much the same way as land grasses retard soil erosion;
- providing habitat for many fish, crustaceans, and shellfish;
- providing food for many marine mammals in and of themselves as well as through the smaller organisms that live on their leaves;
- and most importantly by providing a nursery area for much of Florida's recreationally and commercially important marine life.

Seagrass leaves provide excellent protection for young marine animals from larger open-water predators. Some animals, including manatees, eat the seagrass blades. Still others derive nutrition from eating algae and small animals that colonize the seagrass leaves. The colonizing organisms provide an additional link in the marine food chain.

A young queen conch grazing in a bed of turtle grass. Photo credit: National Oceanic and Atmospheric Administration.

Close-up of turtle grass blades. Photo credit: Paige Gill, Florida Keys National Marine Sanctuary.

MANGROVES

Three species of mangrove trees are found in Florida: red, black and white mangroves. All have adaptations that allow them to thrive in areas that are at least occasionally flooded with salt water. Red mangroves, which grow the furthest out into the water, have special "prop roots" which stabilize the plant even during hurricanes. Mangroves trap and cycle various organic materials, chemical elements, and important nutrients throughout the larger ecosystem. Mangrove roots act not only as physical traps for sediments and other matter, but provide attachment surfaces for various marine organisms. Many of these attached organisms filter water through their bodies and, in turn, trap and cycle nutrients.

Red mangroves. The many "stems" reaching out of the water are actually prop roots. Photo credit: Maia McGuire.

Many small fish seek shelter beneath red mangroves. Photo credit: Carrie Vonderhaar, Ocean Futures Society.

The relationship between mangroves and their associated marine life cannot be over-emphasized. Mangroves provide protected nursery areas for fishes, crustaceans, and shellfish. They also provide food for a multitude of marine species such as snook, snapper, tarpon, jack, sheepshead, red drum, oyster, and shrimp. Florida's important recreational and commercial fisheries will decline without healthy mangrove forests to support them.

Many animals find shelter either in the roots or branches of mangroves. Mangrove branches are rookeries, or nesting areas, for beautiful coastal birds such as brown pelicans and roseate spoonbills.

White ibis and roseate spoonbills in front of red mangroves. Photo credit: Maia McGuire

In South Florida, it's estimated 74 percent of game fish and 90 percent of commercially valuable sea life depend on mangrove forests for some stage of their life cycle. Naturally occurring along many fringing tropical coastlines around the world, these trees also buffer shores from extreme weather and storm erosion. In the Florida Keys, as much as 60 percent of shallow water mangroves have disappeared. It's part of an alarming worldwide trend where nearly 50 percent of the planet's mangrove forests have already been destroyed and of those still remaining, 50 percent are considered to be in poor condition. Some mangrove losses occur naturally as a result of hurricanes, but for the past hundred years, agriculture, mariculture, land clearing for urban development, and mosquito abatement have been the leading causes of their demise.

Aerial Image of Mangrove Creek in Upper Keys. Photo credit: Amy Massey, Florida Keys National Marine Sanctuary.

CULTURAL RESOURCES

The Florida Keys National Marine Sanctuary's submerged cultural resources are unique, non-renewable remnants of the Keys' colorful maritime past. The FKNMS has an extensive education and volunteer program in submerged cultural resources. Volunteers on the Submerged Resources Inventory Team have documented over 400 underwater historical sites in the Sanctuary. The three-volume inventory entitled "Underwater Resources of the Florida Keys National Marine Sanctuary" has been compiled by Mr. Chuck Hayes and is available in public libraries throughout the Florida Keys. The education team has also developed a historic Shipwreck Trail[1] which highlights nine historic vessels that sank in Sanctuary waters. Brochures and underwater site guides for each vessel have been distributed to area dive operators and are also available in three Sanctuary offices.

SHIPWRECK TRAIL

A trail of nine historic shipwrecks is scattered along the treacherous coral reefs and buried in the sandy shallows a few miles off the Florida Keys, and these wrecks have many tales to tell. They can tell us about individuals who came before us, why they were here, and their difficulty in navigating these waters.

One of the goals of the National Marine Sanctuary System is to provide opportunities for people to learn about our rich maritime heritage. Through the Shipwreck Trail, the

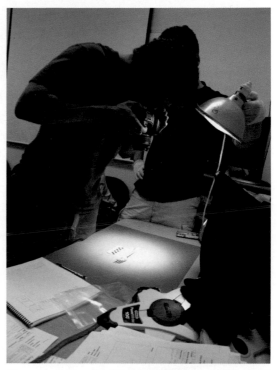

Documentation of artifacts from the 1733 Coffins Patch collection by student archaeologists. Photo credit: Brenda Altmeier, Florida Keys National Marine Sanctuary.

Cable reel on the Thunderbolt shipwreck, which lies in 120 feet of water. The ship, which was built to tend to defensive mines during WWII, is one of nine ships on the sanctuary's Shipwreck Trail. Photo credit: Florida Keys National Marine Sanctuary.

---

1   http://floridakeys.noaa.gov/sanctuary_resources/shipwreck_trail/welcome.html

Wreckage of the Adelaide Baker, a 3-masted wooden sailing ship built in 1863. The wreckage is covered with sea fans, sponges and other marine life. The Adelaide Baker is one of the nine ships on the sanctuary's Shipwreck Trail. Photo credit: Florida Keys National Marine Sanctuary.

Shipwrecks become homes to schools of fish like these grunts and snappers. Photo credit: Florida Keys National Marine Sanctuary.

Florida Keys National Marine Sanctuary is seeking to make this more visible and to encourage an appreciation and understanding of these irreplaceable remnants of our past. The diversity of sites and locations covered by this project provide something of interest for everyone. While teaching about our nation's history and maritime culture, the Shipwreck Trail also helps divert diving pressure from the major natural reefs. Not only do historians, biologists, and anglers seek out these shipwrecks, so do fish! Shipwrecks become artificial reefs, providing a special setting for the brightly colored tropical fish to perform their nature-choreographed water ballets.

Key species within the Sanctuary

ELKHORN AND STAGHORN CORALS

In 2006, NOAA Fisheries Service added branching elkhorn and staghorn corals to the endangered species list as threatened species as these corals were determined "likely to become in danger of extinction throughout all or a significant portion of their range in the foreseeable future." These corals are found typically in shallow water on reefs throughout the Bahamas, Florida and the Caribbean. They live in high-energy zones, with a lot of wave action. Too much wave action (major storms) can cause branching corals to break. However, fragmentation via branch breakage is one method of reproduction for branching corals.

There are many stresses affecting elkhorn and staghorn corals, both natural and human-induced. Land-based sources of pollution, such as runoff, sewage discharge, dredging and coastal development can increase nutrient levels, sediment loading and turbidity. Runoff can also reduce oxygen levels and possibly introduce pathogens. Excess nutrients allow large fleshy algae (macroalgae) to proliferate and overgrow corals. Pathogens may cause diseases in corals such as white-band disease and white pox/patchy necrosis, which are thought to be two of the most significant causes of mortality to elkhorn and staghorn corals. Climate change, associated with increased water temperature and elevated light levels, may cause bleaching, reduced coral growth rates and deposition rate of their calcium carbonate skeleton.

Elkhorn coral (top) and staghorn coral (bottom). Photo credits: Florida Keys National Marine Sanctuary.

Elkhorn coral. Photo credit: Bill Precht, Florida Keys National Marine Sanctuary.

Overfishing and disease have caused a reduction in the number of important predatory fishes such as groupers and herbivores (plant eaters) including parrotfish. Reduction in the number of predatory fishes can possibly lead to an increase in organisms that prey on corals, such as the short coral snail, fireworm, and damselfish. Furthermore, without a healthy herbivorous fish population, macroalgae growth limits the recovery of stressed corals and the settlement of new baby corals to replace those that have been lost from disease, bleaching, predation and overgrowth. Elkhorn and staghorn corals are particularly sensitive to sediment, as they are among the least effective of the reef-building corals at trapping and removing sediment from their surface. Because they live in shallow water, elkhorn and staghorn corals may be exposed to excessive ultraviolet (UV) light which can lead to bleaching.

Queen parrotfish swimming at the reef. Photo credit: Florida Keys National Marine Sanctuary.

WEST INDIAN MANATEE

The West Indian or Florida manatee is a mammal that can live in both fresh and salt water. Manatees have a large, bulky, rounded body that tapers into a round, paddle-like tail. Their two front flippers help the animal maneuver in the water and move food towards its mouth. Its gray skin is thin and wrinkly, and it has powerful lips that dig for food. The average adult manatee is about 10 feet long and weighs about 1000 pounds. Manatees rely completely on plants for their food source, consuming about 100 pounds per day. Manatees, along with their relatives in the order Sirenia, are the only herbivorous marine mammals in the world.

West Indian manatee. Photo credit: Kip Evans.

West Indian manatees in the United States are protected under federal law by the Marine Mammal Protection Act of 1972, and the Endangered Species Act of 1973, which make it illegal to harass, hunt, capture, or kill any marine mammal. West Indian manatees are also protected by the Florida Manatee Sanctuary Act of 1978. Manatees are mammals, so they must surface to breathe air. It is while surfacing that manatees are most vulnerable to being hit by watercraft.

The biggest threats to manatees are human-related, with watercraft strikes and entanglement in marine debris topping the list. Cold weather and red tide events are two natural occurrences that result in high manatee mortalities in some years.

GOLIATH GROUPER

The goliath grouper is colored brown to olive-green with dark spots over its body and fins. The largest fish found around reefs, it can grow to 8 feet in length and weigh more than 800 pounds. This species is known to grow slowly and live up to 37 years. Adult goliath grouper live between 10-100 feet deep, around ledges, wrecks and caves. They are occasionally found on coral reefs. Juvenile goliath grouper live close to shore around mangroves for up to six years. By the time they reach about 3 feet (1 meter) in length, these fish have moved offshore to their adult habitat. In late July, mature goliath groupers migrate to their spawning areas, which might be hundreds of miles from their home territory. They finish spawning by the end of October. The goliath grouper used to be fairly common but has been greatly reduced due to overfishing. The population has shown some signs of recovery since this species was first protected from fishing in 1990. In the past, hundreds of grouper would gather in a single spawning location, recently the highest number recorded has been 65.

Two goliath grouper in a school of smaller fishes. Goliath groupers can weigh up to 800 pounds and reach eight feet long. Photo credit: Carrie Vonderhaar, Ocean Futures Society.

Goliath groupers were once abundant in all of the coastal waters of Florida. Encounters with these creatures had never drifted far from our memories, those lurking hulks that would silently, suddenly, materialize beside us, their dark forms always larger than our own. In spite of our dive training, their presence had the power to quell the breath and paralyze the brain. They can reach eight feet long and 800 pounds and are known to live around the deepwater wrecks, sink holes and natural ledges that offer both protection and positions from which to ambush their prey. Sensational stories of these giant fish stalking incautious divers aren't new. There are anecdotes that span decades, back to when the goliaths were called Jewfish and underwater hunters would recount harrowing tales, some possibly true and others more likely "fish stories," of limbs being swallowed and of spear guns being ripped free from their grasp.

Goliath grouper in the Tortugas Ecological Reserve. Photo credit: Carrie Vonderhaar, Ocean Futures Society.

As we began to learn more about the life history of these giant fish though, such stories seemed less surprising. Goliath groupers are sovereigns of their home territories and that can at times apparently include claiming ownership to anyone else's speared fish. Combative encounters with the deepwater behemoths are in fact, quite rare. But news reports of attacks occasionally grab headlines and the giant fish is usually fingered for being at fault. But when the "real facts" surface, it's usually the bad behavior of divers that provoke goliath grouper attacks. Consumer demand for these fish has led to over-harvesting and like most other large grouper species around the world, they have nearly disappeared.

The fabled spawning aggregations of hundreds of goliath grouper have dwindled since the early 1980s. And some have disappeared altogether. The giants still congregate in late August and early September, but now, they are only found around deepwater wrecks, including some off the Tortugas.

"Mangroves may be the bottleneck to the survival of the giant fish," Felicia Coleman[2] explains to us. Protection from fishing may have halted the goliath groupers' slide towards extinction, but a deeper understanding of their complex life cycle is revealing the importance of also preserving their habitat. For goliaths, that can mean many locations associated with many different stages of life. From the spawning sites near the deep wrecks of the Tortugas, the ritual of courtship results in the climax of one synchronized moment where the goliaths cast their sperm and eggs into the sea. Larvae emerge

Two juvenile goliath groupers hide among the roots of mangrove trees in the Florida Keys National Marine Sanctuary. Photo credit: Carrie Vonderhaar, Ocean Futures Society.

from fertilized eggs to drift at the mercy of ocean currents, eyes and mouths develop along the way, and these small specks of life enter the food chain. After about a month, the translucent larvae are carried towards shore and settle in among the roots of mangrove trees where they transform into juvenile groupers, complete miniatures of the adults in color, pattern and shape, except they are only one inch long. Felicia points out that if they manage to survive the gauntlet of predatory obstacles in the

2   Dr. Felicia C. Coleman is the director of Florida State University's Coastal and Marine Laboratory, and a professor in the school's Department of Biological Science.

open sea, the baby goliaths will die upon arrival to a shoreline devoid of mangrove trees. Like numbers of species of fish, invertebrates, birds, and even some mammals, baby goliaths depend on mangroves for food and shelter.

In addition to healthy trees, juvenile goliaths also need good water quality to survive. In South Florida, agriculture and urban water resource needs have dramatically altered the volume and quality of fresh water that historically flowed from the Everglades into Florida Bay. Pesticides enter mangrove nurseries and agricultural nutrients reduce the amount of available oxygen, while artificial management of water flow creates salinity fluctuations beyond the juvenile's abilities to internally moderate. This compounded degradation of the environment is what Felicia describes as a "death by a thousand cuts," to underscore how the slow eating away of essential habitat may impact the recovery of an endangered species. But based on data from their tagging studies, scientists are cautiously optimistic that the goliaths are on the track to a slow recovery. Therein lies a conundrum. Without information describing the original size of

populations, disagreements over how many goliaths constitute recovery are starting to arise.

Felicia explains the complexities. "A lot of fishermen argue that the goliath grouper are eating all the other smaller snappers and that we should open up protection and start harvesting them so that we can get the snapper back. We argue that maybe the reason the goliath are there is because they've been protected for almost 15 years and the reason the other fish are gone is that they have been fished out. But you always need data to back those things

Goliath groupers gather on deepwater wrecks in the Tortugas Ecological Reserve. Photo credit: Carrie Vonderhaar, Ocean Futures Society.

up," she says. Comparisons of fish sizes and abundance within and outside no-take reserves are one way scientists can help make those determinations.

It's not that the groupers were trying to get away from us because we were watching them mate. I think it was that they needed to be away from the wreck so that females could release their eggs and the males could release their sperm in the currents, which flow in a very specific direction, toward the mangroves over 100 miles away. It tells us how critical those mangroves are: they play a vital role for the reproduction of many, many species, and especially for the grouper, whose few eggs will make it into adulthood. After fertilization, the groupers' eggs hatch into larvae that drift with the currents for about six weeks then transform into bottom dwellers and settle into the mangroves for protection, the right temperature, food. They will spend five or six years of their life there before they leave. Without the mangroves, there will be no significant recovery of the groupers. One has to realize how everything's connected. And the groupers are just one species; but they help us to understand how all species have some sort of critical connection with their environment.

Emerging Environmental Issues

FIBROPAPILLOMATOSIS

Fibropapillomatosis (FP) is a tumor-forming disease that affects sea turtles around the world. First described in captured adult green turtles (*Chelonia mydas*) in the 1930s, it was later identified in mariculture-reared green turtles at Cayman Turtle Farm, Grand Cayman, B.W.I. in the late 1970s. In the 1980s, the prevalence started increasing at multiple sites including Florida and Hawaii where more than 50 percent of certain populations were found to be affected. While green turtles were the first marine turtle identified with FP, similar tumors have been found in loggerhead, hawksbill, Kemp's ridley and olive ridley sea turtles. High prevalence areas are shallow near-shore waters with relatively restricted water turnover. Many (but not all) of these marine habitats are near areas of heavy human use. The actual cause of this disease is unknown, but a herpes-like virus has been found in association with the tumors. The disease is known to be highly infectious and is easily transmitted from turtle to turtle. While there is no way to treat turtles with internal tumors, external tumors have been successfully removed by using laser surgery.

Despite all of the beautiful images etched in our minds from this expedition, we won't forget that sterile room, or the unmistakable odor of cauterized tissue and the withering cast of tungsten lamps. "You're going to be cutting these tumors out of her eyes?" Fabien asked. "Right," explained Dr. Mader.[3] "You can see . . . right here on the eyelid, these are little papilloma tumors." Florida's green sea turtles are in a bad way. Sixty to seventy percent of juvenile greens are affected by this deadly, transmissible disease, fibropapillomatosis (FP), a tumor-forming virus.

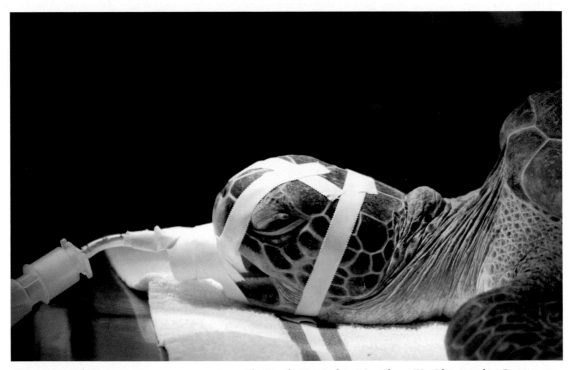

Green sea turtle in surgery to remove tumors at The Turtle Hospital in Marathon, FL. Photo credit: Carrie Vonderhaar, Ocean Futures Society.

---

3   Dr. Doug Mader is the consulting veterinarian at The Turtle Hospital in Marathon, FL

"If you look very carefully, you can see that it's not obscuring her vision. One of the sad things about this disease is the disease itself doesn't actually kill the turtles," Dr. Mader explains. But "if that tumor gets big enough she could go blind, and then, sadly starve to death." Tumors may also manifest in a turtle's mouth, lungs, kidneys, and flippers, sometimes reaching the size of grapefruits. "You can imagine what that does to the hydrodynamics and their ability to swim," Dr. Mader reflects.

PANDEMICS

While pandemic diseases are not new, many scientists agree the pace of outbreaks is accelerating. Emerging infectious diseases (EIDs) are by their nature defined by increases in their occurrence, expanded ranges and discovery in other species. Chinese horseshoe bats have been linked to the origins of severe acute respiratory syndrome, or SARS, while Ebola, Lyme disease, AIDS, and potentially, bird flu, are all believed to have moved from wildlife to human populations.

Why are these deadly pathogens hopping barriers they had never breached before? According to a group of research scientists and medical doctors that reported their collaborative findings in Environmental Health Perspectives, the answer rests squarely with us. Human-induced land use changes, like deforestation, agricultural encroachment, road construction, dams, and the expansion of urban environments are, according to this consortium, the primary drivers of infectious disease outbreaks. And in the case of the fibropapilloma virus, while the exact cause is still unknown, research is connecting a high prevalence of tumors to heavily polluted coasts.

For conservationists, it's an uncomfortably familiar place that often leads to the question of how preserving the environment can ever be balanced with a human population's increasing demand for more resources. While the answers are not necessarily easy, they do exist.

INVASIVE SPECIES—LIONFISH

Lionfish, not native to the Atlantic Ocean, are increasing in abundance in these waters. Photo credit: National Oceanic and Atmospheric Administration.

Like many regions in the western Atlantic, the Florida Keys National Marine Sanctuary has been colonized by non-native lionfish. Lionfish are members of the scorpionfish family and are native to the Indo-Pacific Ocean. Since 2000, scientists have become aware of growing populations of lionfish in the Atlantic Ocean. Original sightings of these striking striped fish, with their showy fins, were made on reefs off the coast of Florida, South Carolina, North Carolina and Bermuda. Since that time, the fish have spread throughout the

Western Atlantic Ocean. A map showing reported lionfish sightings is available at the US Geological Survey's nuisance aquatic species website.[4]

Researchers have several concerns about the increasing abundance of lionfish in the Atlantic. As with any non-native species that becomes established, there is a fear that lionfish will compete with native fish for food and space. Gut content analyses of lionfish that have been captured in the Atlantic reveal that their prey items include juvenile grouper and cleaner fish (like wrasses). Published data show that single lionfish transplanted onto small patch reefs reduce recruitment of native fishes by nearly 80 percent on those reefs. In their native waters, lionfish are eaten by cornetfish, however they have few predators in the Atlantic.

Holly Lohuis checks out a young lionfish in its native habitat in Papua New Guinea. Photo credit: Carrie Vonderhaar, Ocean Futures Society.

4   http://nas.er.usgs.gov/taxgroup/fish/lionfishdistribution.asp

How did lionfish get into the Atlantic Ocean? It seems that the most likely pathway was through escape or release of aquarium fish. Several lionfish are thought to have escaped into Miami waters when some beachfront home and business aquaria were destroyed by Hurricane Andrew in 1992. Others may have been intentionally released by aquarium hobbyists who believed that they were doing a good thing for the lionfish by releasing them into the ocean. There is also a very slight possibility that lionfish larvae may have been transported into waters of the coastal US through shipping transport (in ballast water). Whatever the initial introduction method, ocean currents seem to be responsible for the distribution of lionfish from the southeastern US states throughout the greater Caribbean region, Bermuda and even New England (where they apparently do not survive the winter months.)

Lionfish have venomous spines on three types of fins. There are 13 venomous spines on the dorsal (back) fin, one on each of the pelvic fins (front, bottom fins) and three on the anal fin (underside of the body near the tail). The pectoral (side) fins and caudal (tail) fin do not have spines. Since lionfish are not shy, and tend to keep their fins spread out even if divers approach them, divers can become stung by these spines if they are not careful. The sting from a lionfish spine is comparable to that of a stingray's barb. Treatment is also similar— the affected body part should be submerged in hot (not scalding) water to denature the toxin. Aspirin pain relievers can also be used. Affected people should receive medical attention as soon as possible. Symptoms of a lionfish sting can include intense throbbing and sharp pain, redness and swelling around the wound, a tingling sensation around the wound for days to weeks, sweating and blistering, headaches, nausea or vomiting, and even seizures. If left untreated, there is a chance of breathing and heart complications, or abdominal pain and paralysis.

Adult lionfish. Photo credit: Maia McGuire.

Lionfish have occasionally been caught by fishermen, but this is an infrequent occurrence. Anglers should be cautious when attempting to remove these fish from their hooks. Lionfish should NOT be released back into the ocean if caught. The fish are actually edible, and are valued as a food fish in many parts of their natural range. The toxins in the spines are not released into the meat of the fish, so there is nothing "poisonous" about the fish. Lionfish are considered "venomous" (like stingrays or catfish), while fish like pufferfish, which contain toxins in their muscle are considered "poisonous" and should not be eaten. Anglers wishing to prepare lionfish for cooking should cut off the venomous spines before cleaning the fish to avoid becoming envenomated ("stung").

Lionfish are generally found around reefs or other structures in depths from 4-450 feet. They mature early, may reproduce year-round and, in the Atlantic, can grow to be about 18 inches in length. Divers and anglers are asked to report lionfish sightings to the USGS nuisance aquatic species hotline by calling 877-STOP-ANS (877-786-7267) or reporting online.[5]

Research within the Sanctuary

Research projects within the sanctuary system allow scientists to better understand the ecosystem and how it functions within a sanctuary. Research also allows scientists to better understand the resources within a sanctuary and how their condition is affected and changed. Scientists will also create models to represent ecosystems. Managers can then use these models to predict future changes and make appropriate preventative actions or purposeful restoration efforts. Recent research studies in the Florida Keys National Marine Sanctuary include the following:

- Coral ecology—Projects focus on the feeding and reproduction of coral as well as factors affecting reef erosion.
- Coral disease and bleaching—Researchers are looking at different types of bleaching and disease and the effects of ultraviolet light on bleaching, and the growth of algae on reefs.
- Water quality—Efforts include looking into the production and release of nutrients from reefs, the impact of contaminants on Florida Bay water, and the effects of currents and upwelling.
- Fish ecology—Scientific studies include lobster spawning and reproduction, size of fish populations, and fish disease.

---

5   http://nas.er.usgs.gov

A partially-bleached brain coral. Photo credit: Richard Murphy, Ocean Futures Society.

Spiny lobster. Photo credit: Florida Keys National Marine Sanctuary.

Visiting the Sanctuary

Note: In the last section of the book, "When You Visit the Sanctuaries," is detailed information about resources found within each sanctuary to help visitors have an enjoyable and productive visit.

VISITOR'S CENTER
Florida Keys Eco-Discovery Center
35 East Quay Road, Key West, FL 33040
Located at the end of Southard Street in Truman Annex in Key West, across the street from Fort Zachary Taylor Historic State Park

Open Tuesday - Saturday
9 a.m. - 4 p.m.
(Closed on Thanksgiving and Christmas)
Admission is free
Telephone: 305-809-4750

The National Oceanic and Atmospheric Administration (NOAA) opened the doors to its 6,400-square-foot Florida Keys Eco-Discovery Center in 2007, treating visitors to an exciting array of interactive exhibits highlighting the rich natural environment of the Keys. The center offers free admission and a fun, educational experience for visitors of all ages.

Entrance to the Sanctuary's Visitor's Center in Key West. Photo credit: Craig Wanous, Florida Keys National Marine Sanctuary.

Located in NOAA's Dr. Nancy Foster Florida Keys Environmental Complex on the Truman Annex waterfront in Key West, the center features numerous exhibits that interpret the resources and management efforts of Florida Keys National Marine Sanctuary, two national parks, and four national wildlife refuges. Highlights include a simulation of the Aquarius underwater habitat, where scientists (called "aquanauts") live sixty feet underwater during ten-day research missions. The simulation is complete with sights and sounds experienced by the "aquanauts", and a high-definition theater screening a 17-minute video about Florida Keys National Marine Sanctuary by world-renowned filmmaker Bob Talbot.

EcoDiscovery Aquarius mock-up. Photo credit: Florida Keys National Marine Sanctuary.

Visitors can also peer through an underwater camera to watch the spectacle of coral spawning, learn about the arma-

A visitor checks out the EcoDiscovery Camera. Photo credit: Florida Keys National Marine Sanctuary.

The coral reef exhibit at the Visitor's Center. Photo Credit: Craig Wanous, Florida Keys National Marine Sanctuary.

ments that once defended remote Fort Jefferson, or take a journey through the natural habitats of south Florida, from the Everglades to teeming coral reefs.

The center was developed by the National Oceanic and Atmospheric Administration, the United States Fish and Wildlife Service, the National Park Service, and the South Florida Water Management District. Other agencies and organizations that are represented in the center include NOAA's National Weather Service and National Geodetic Survey; the Florida Department of Environmental Protection; and the Florida Fish and Wildlife Conservation Commission; and Mote Marine Laboratory, which utilizes live aquarium displays to educate the public on coral reef natural history, research, and conservation efforts. Eastern National Foundation, a National Park Service cooperating association, operates a small museum store, the profits from which benefit the center.

The Center also offers an interactive, 3-D topographic/bathymetric map of the entire Sanctuary. Visitors can choose several different features located throughout the Sanctuary to highlight on the map

Regional administrative offices are located in two additional locations:

UPPER REGIONAL OFFICE

95230 Overseas Highway
Key Largo, FL 33037
305-852-7717

ECO-TOURS

Whether interested in bird watching, wildlife viewing, or simply boating in the splendid aquamarine waters of the Keys, there are plenty of options for eco-friendly encounters with the rich and varied habitats of the Sanctuary. Low tide is the best time to see wading birds or to see sharks, bonefish, stingrays taking advantage of fish exposed on the shallow flats and tide pools. Midday is the best time to look for fish. The direct sunlight penetrates the clear waters and allows you to see colorful fish, corals and sponges. Four major marine ecosystems provide a variety of habitat viewing: coral reef, mangrove, seagrass beds, and hardbottom (sponge beds). For an educational and personally rewarding experience, coastal cleanups are a great way to make new friends and help our fragile environment.

A volunteer collects trash in the Sanctuary. Photo credit: Florida Keys National Marine Sanctuary.

BOATING

Dotted with anchorages and harbors throughout the hundreds of islands, there are many opportunities for sailing and boating in the Florida Keys National Marine Sanctuary. The warm sun and gentle climate, coupled with breathtaking sunsets set the stage for a dream experience enjoyed at its best on the water. Essentially, any and all types of boats are available for rental throughout the Florida Keys and can be delivered to your dock or door. Boating and sailing schools offer lessons, classes, charters, and clubs. Certified instruction is available from both the U.S. Sailing and American Sailing Associations.

There are many public boat ramps available throughout the Florida Keys. Boaters planning to visit the Sanctuary are encouraged to first read the free Sanctuary brochures (available online[6] or at Sanctuary offices) to find locations of boat ramps, mooring buoys and restricted zones. To avoid disturbing wildlife, boaters are encouraged to stay 100 yards or more offshore; and to keep speed, noise and wakes to a minimum near mangroves.

Kayaking is a great way to explore nearshore waters. Photo credit: Nancy Diersing, Florida Keys National Marine Sanctuary.

---

6   http://floridakeys.noaa.gov/edu/FKNMS_lower_region.pdf and http://floridakeys.noaa.gov/edu/FKNMS_upper_region.pdf

Some areas of the Florida Keys National Marine Sanctuary are designated as Special-use Research Only areas. Access to these areas is prohibited without a research permit from the Sanctuary. These areas are in the vicinity of Conch Reef, Tennessee Reef, Looe Key Patch Reef and Eastern Sambo. Vessels may enter the South Tortugas Ecological Reserve, but must remain in continuous transit with fishing gear stowed. Anchoring is prohibited in Ecological Reserves (Western Sambo, North Tortugas) and within Sanctuary Preservation Areas when mooring buoys are available. See diving section below for additional information about the North Tortugas Ecological Reserve.

Boat tied to a mooring buoy within the Sanctuary. Photo credit: Carrie Vonderhaar, Ocean Futures Society.

There are several Wildlife Management Areas within the Sanctuary. These are marked with signs and may have special restrictions including no-wake zones, and limited closures. Boaters should pay close attention to signs in these areas. Personal watercraft and airboats are illegal in all National Parks and Wildlife Refuges in the Florida Keys. Camping, campfires and collecting of any kind are prohibited on all National Wildlife Refuges.

Before heading out, boaters should check weather conditions. Strong winds and rough seas can result in poor visibility and reduce safe interaction at the reef. Dumping trash at sea is illegal; plastic bags and other debris can injure or kill marine animals. Boaters should plan to bring trash back to shore and recycle it. This includes fishing gear and equipment, especially monofilament line.

Waterspout off Key West dock. Photo credit: Todd Hitchins, Florida Keys National Marine Sanctuary.

State waters within the Florida Keys National Marine Sanctuary (up to 3 miles from shore) are designated as a "No Discharge Zone." This means that it is illegal to discharge sewage (black water), whether treated or not treated in these waters. Boaters should use sewage pumpout facilities (available at many marinas in the Keys) and biodegradable bilge cleaner and never discharge bilgewater at the reef.

Many boaters do not realize that coral reefs and seagrass beds in the Florida Keys can be growing within inches of the water's surface whether they are located close to shore or several miles offshore. In the period between 1980 and 1993, approximately 500 vessels were reported aground in the Looe Key and Key Largo Sanctuaries. However, an additional 500 groundings were documented in the Florida Keys NMS between July 1993 and June 1994.

These groundings have a cumulative effect on the resources. Over 19 acres of coral reef habitat has been damaged or destroyed by large ship groundings. Boat propellers have damaged over 30,000 acres of seagrasses. Direct impacts to resources also result from careless divers and snorkelers standing on coral, improperly placed anchors, and destructive fishing methods.

Prop scars in seagrass beds alongside the channel markers show the importance of following the marked channels. Photo credit: Carrie Vonderhaar, Ocean Futures Society.

Boaters should consult tide and navigational charts and steer clear of shallow areas. To prevent damage to coral or seagrasses, please use reef mooring buoys or anchor in sandy areas away from coral and seagrass beds. Remember that fines can be imposed for damage to corals or seagrasses. The Sanctuary encourages boaters to pay attention to the color of the water to help prevent accidental groundings and damage to these habitats.

Remember, "<u>Brown</u>, brown, run aground. <u>White</u>, white, you might. <u>Green</u>, green, nice and clean. <u>Blue</u>, blue, sail on through."

- Reef formations that grow close to the water's surface and shallow sea grass beds will make the water appear brown. Such areas should be avoided to keep from running aground and damaging both your boat and these sensitive habitats.
- Sand bars and shallow rubble areas appear white. These areas can be deceiving and may be much shallower than they appear. Navigate with caution around these areas.
- Green water usually indicates areas free of shallow reefs or seagrass beds. Navigation of small, shallow draft boats in these areas is generally safe. However, larger, shallow draft boats should exercise caution. All boaters should carry and consult the appropriate NOAA marine chart.
- Deep-water areas, such as the ocean side of a reef may appear blue. Navigation in these areas is free from hazardous contact with reefs or seagrass beds. Remember, however, that coral reefs rise abruptly from deep water so give yourself plenty of room to maneuver.

If a boat does run aground, boaters should immediately turn the engine off, and tilt it up if possible. They should not try to motor off. Instead, they should wait until high tide to remove the vessel and call for assistance if necessary.

Paying attention to the color of the water can alert boaters to shallow sandbars, reefs and seagrass beds. Photo credit: Carrie Vonderhaar, Ocean Futures Society.

FISHING

Fishing in the Keys is legendary and may have best been immortalized through the novels of Ernest Hemingway. The Keys hold so many world-class fishing opportunities that it may be difficult to decide which type a person wants to experience. From flats and backcountry to deep sea and offshore fishing, from Key Largo to Key West, there is an opportunity to fit every individual and most every weather situation. Florida law requires a fishing license. Applicable size, bag limits, and seasons must be observed when harvesting seafood and all excess fish must be released. Florida's saltwater fishing regulations can be found at most bait and tackle stores, or online.[7]

---

7   http://www.myfwc.com/Fishing/Index.htm

Jean-Michel Cousteau swims alongside a Nassau grouper, one of many grouper species in the Florida Keys. Photo Credit: Tom Ordway, Ocean Futures Society.

Fishing is not allowed in the North and South Tortugas Ecological Reserves. In Sanctuary Preservation areas, only catch and release fishing by trolling is allowed. These areas include Carysfort Reef, Cheeca Rocks, Elbow, Alligator Reef, Key Largo Dry Rocks, Coffins Patch, Grecian Rocks, Sombrero Key, French Reef, Looe Key, Molasses Reef, Newfound Harbor, Conch Reef, Eastern Dry Rocks, Hen and Chickens, Rock Key, Davis Reef and Sand Key. No-take areas are designated by 30" diameter round buoys. Bait fishing in Sanctuary Preservation Areas is allowed by permit only (contact the Sanctuary for details.) Spearfishing or possession of spearfishing equipment (except while passing through without interruption) is prohibited in the Key Largo and Looe Key management areas.

A fisherman looks for bait. Photo credit: Nancy Diersing, Florida Keys National Marine Sanctuary.

When fishing, boaters need to take care not to troll over or near divers. Boats should stay at least 100 feet from a red and white diver down flag and watch for bubbles. Fishermen should not throw fish carcasses or lobster heads overboard or into canals as they degenerate and degrade water quality.

Boaters should give a wide berth to boats that are flying a "diver down" flag. Photo credit: Carrie Vonderhaar, Ocean Futures Society.

DIVING/SNORKELING

The close proximity to land and an abundance of boat operators in the Keys make the diverse underwater world of the Florida Keys easily accessible for the novice snorkeler and the seasoned diver alike. The sanctuary has been called the most popular diving playground in the United States. Hard corals such as elkhorn, staghorn, pillar, brain and star coral abound. Water temperatures are in the mid-80's in summer and low 70's in winter. Visibility can vary greatly according to weather conditions and other factors but is typically in the 40-60 foot range. When the Gulf Stream moves close to the reefs, visibility can exceed 100 feet. Conditions are best for diving from May to September. Divers may observe dense schools of reef fish, including goatfish, parrotfish and blue tang, as well as lobster, nurse sharks and moray eels. Wreck diving includes the *City of Washington*, *Benwood*, *Bibb* and *Duane*.

Jean-Michel Cousteau observes a barracuda. Photo credit: Tom Ordway, Ocean Futures Society.

Before booking a reef trip, check out weather conditions; it is best not to go out in rough seas. Poor visibility, strong winds and waves reduce safe interaction at the reef. Coral reefs are under increased pressures globally. Through practicing responsible diving and snorkeling, people can help to lessen local stress on the reef while still partaking of its beauty. Remember that even the lightest touch with hands or equipment can damage sensitive coral polyps. People should never stand on a coral reef. Snorkelers should wear float coats — inflatable snorkel vests — to allow gear adjustment without standing on the coral. To avoid contact with the ocean bottom, divers should only use the weight needed and practice proper buoyancy control. Areas that appear empty may support new growth if left undisturbed.

Because the reefs are so shallow, even snorkelers can get a great view of the underwater life there. Photo Credit: Ivy Kelley, Florida Keys National Marine Sanctuary.

Divers and snorkelers should avoid wearing gloves and touching or collecting marine life. Most tropical fish captured die within a year. Queen conch is a protected species, and cannot be taken. People should not feed fish, seabirds and marine mammals; it changes their natural behavior and diet. It is illegal to harvest coral in Florida and buying it at local shops only depletes reefs elsewhere in the world. Boaters should bring any trash back to shore and recycle it, if possible. Snorkel aware, dive with care!

A no-cost permit is required for diving in the northern section of the Tortugas Ecological Reserve. This permit requirement ensures that there will be enough mooring buoy sites for all dive boats visiting the reserve at a given time (anchoring is not allowed in this ecological reserve.)

A diver swims past large star corals and sea rods.
Photo credit: Florida Keys National Marine Sanctuary.

To obtain a dive permit, call 305-292-0311 or 305-743-2437 or visit the Sanctuary office in Key West or Marathon.

Permits must be requested at least 72 hours but no longer than one month before the desired effective date of the permit. The southern portion of the Tortugas Ecological Reserve is more heavily protected; mooring/anchoring, fishing, snorkeling and diving are not allowed there.

Schools of grunts are commonly seen on the reefs.
Photo credit: Florida Keys National Marine Sanctuary.

The partial list on the following pages provides just a glimpse of the multitude of dive destinations within the Sanctuary: Dive sites recommended for novice divers are in pale blue, intermediate sites are in green, and those recommended only for advanced divers are in pink. Some sites have a variety of features; those rated for novice to intermediate are in medium blue, those for intermediate to advanced are orange and those for novice to advanced are in purple.

UPPER KEYS-KEY LARGO DIVE SITES	
TURTLE REEF Depth Range: 25 feet Experience Level: Intermediate	Turtle Reef is located at the northernmost site of the Key Largo Marine Sanctuary, and most reef species are represented here. The site is relatively shallow, and visibility is usually good. The reef's location protects it from the strong currents lying beyond, but it *is* influenced by tidal currents passing through Hawk Channel.
CARYSFORT REEF Depth Range: 35-70 feet Experience Level: Intermediate	Because of its distance from the more central dive sites, comparatively few divers visit Carysfort Reef. This site has exceptional beauty and offers a variety of options from shallow to deep dives. The shallow upper section of the reef abounds with marine life and is perfect for snorkelers.
CARYSFORT SOUTH Depth Range: 20 feet Experience Level: Intermediate	A natural extension of Carysfort Reef, Carysfort South is similar in its configuration and displays a double reef structure. Its famous elkhorn coral gardens make this reef a highly attractive location. South of the reef lie the remains of the H.M.S. Winchester, a 933-ton British man-of-war that sank in 1695 after running aground on the reef.
THE ELBOW Depth Range: 12-35 feet Experience Level: Novice	Named for its angular shape, The Elbow is a classic example of spurs and grooves which meander down the slope of the reef. The coral fingers are extremely well-defined and are separated by level passages of clean sand; some of the spurs are high enough to be considered mini-walls. Corals and fish abound here but wrecks hold the secret to this site's appeal. The Civil War Wreck, a 752-ton steamer sunk in 1866 has lovely fingers of elkhorn coral situated at depths of 6-18 feet. The remains of two more wrecks, probably a tug and a barge are also scattered in this area.

KEY LARGO DRY ROCKS Depth Range: Shallow to 25 feet Experience Level: Novice	By far the most famous dive in the Key Largo Marine Sanctuary, the Statue of Christ of the Abyss (also known as Christ of the Deep), rests on a concrete base located within a short canyon at Key Largo Dry Rocks. This area is celebrated for its marvelous specimens of brain coral and the eastern side of the reef displays classic coral fingers which are rich in marine life. This area also includes Grecian Rocks, an extremely popular reef among snorkelers.
GRECIAN ROCKS Depth Range: Shallow to 25 feet Experience Level: Novice	Grecian Rocks is an exceptionally popular reef for snorkelers. The grass and sand on the back side provide good anchorage, and the shallow reef buffers the waves so the waters are very calm even on windy days. It is very easy for snorkelers to swim from the boat up to the reef line where the corals and brightly colored fish abound.
THE CHRIST OF THE ABYSS STATUE Depth: 25 feet Experience Level: Novice	The Christ Statue was cast in Italy and donated to the Underwater Society of America by Egidi Cressi, an Italian industrialist and diving equipment manufacturer. It is a 9 foot tall bronze duplicate of the Christ of the Abysses statue, which stands in 50 feet of water off Genoa, Italy. Set in a beautiful reef area known for its outstanding brain corals, the figure of Christ stands silhouetted against the blue waters of the ocean, His arms upraised to the surface. This dramatic and memorable picture is one that most diving visitors to the Keys shouldn't miss.
THE BENWOOD Depth Range: 50 feet offshore, 20 feet inshore Experience Level: Novice to Intermediate	An English built cargo vessel lost in a tragic chain of events in 1942, the Benwood rests on a level expanse of sand noticeably lacking in coral growth. Apart from the wreck itself there is comparatively little to see at this location. The ship's fractured stern lies directly beneath the marker at a depth of 2 feet, while its bow points offshore at a depth of 45 feet. The bow section looms up out of the sand, in contrast with the rest of the ship which is almost wholly submerged.
FRENCH REEF Depth Range: Shallow to 100 feet Experience Level: Novice to Advanced	An exceptionally beautiful site, the ever popular French Reef is crammed full of caves, canyons, ledges, tunnels and swim-throughs. This reef is home to a wide variety of fish species.

BLUE HOLE Depth Range: 30-70 feet Experience Level: Intermediate	A relatively deep site, Blue Hole slopes gently from 30 feet down to the 70-foot deep sandy seafloor. To find the Blue Hole itself, look for two sand chutes running from the slope of the reef to its base; south of the chutes a type of mound thrusts its way upwards out of a deep canyon. The seafloor is of clean sand, without the well-developed staghorn and elkhorn colonies observed elsewhere.
MOLASSES REEF Depth Range: Shallow to 40 feet Experience Level: Novice to Intermediate	The world's most popular dive site, Molasses Reef comprises a classic spur and groove system which begins near the surface and falls gradually to a depth of 55 feet. It is washed by the Gulf Stream, so visibility is usually excellent. Impressive concentrations of marine flora and fauna cover just about the entire tropical reef spectrum.
BIBB & DUANE Depth Range: 50-130 feet Experience Level: Advanced	Twin 327-foot coast guard cutters were painstakingly sunk in 1987 as part of an artificial reef program sponsored by the Keys Association of Dive Operators. The Duane, more frequently dived because of her depth, lies upright with a slight list to starboard at a depth of about 100 feet. The Bibb overturned while sinking and lies on her starboard side; you will begin to reach the ship's exterior at a depth of 95 feet. Both ships are equally-rewarding dives with fascinating histories. Because this site is prone to extremely powerful currents, people have to occasionally postpone their dives here.
SPIEGEL GROVE Depth Range: 45 to 130 feet Experience Level: Advanced	Sunk June 10, 2002, the Spiegel Grove is the largest vessel intentionally sunk to make an artificial reef. The ship was designed to carry cargo and craft for amphibious landings, and was retired by the Navy in 1989. After more than three years resting on its starboard side, waves from Hurricane Dennis pushed this 510-foot U.S. Navy ship into an upright position, before the hurricane brushed the Florida Keys in 2005.

ISLAMORADA DIVE SITES

PICKLES REEF Depth Range: 10-25 feet Experience Level: Novice to Intermediate	An elongated reef with familiar spurs and grooves configurations, Pickles Reef is an excellent place for a second dive. The combination of shallow reef and sandy seafloor is full of possibilities for excellent macro photography.
CONCH REEF Depth Range: Shallow to 100 feet Experience Level: Novice to Advanced	The most remarkable aspect of Conch Reef is its proliferation of barrel sponges covering much of the reef area; the second is its depth. The upper section of the slope lies at an average depth of 50 feet., but its base extends to 90 feet. where a wide strip of sand running parallel to the reef lends added definition to its contours. You will observe a variety of gorgonians and reef species, and thanks to the depth it is not unusual to view pelagic fish.
LITTLE CONCH REEF Depth Range: 30 feet Experience Level: Intermediate	A level, comparatively long reef full of coral heads, rocks, low profile spurs and grooves, Little Conch Reef is crisscrossed by ledges, especially in its western section. Tube sponges and seafan colonies grace the area.
THE SAN JOSE AND THE INFANTE Depth Range: 12-15 feet Experience Level: Novice	Two galleons belonging to the famous Silver Plate Fleet of 1733 were lost in a hurricane off the Keys and went down within a mile of one another. Not much is left of the Infante except some timber planking originally from the ship's deck and ballast stones of all shapes and sizes scattered over roughly an acre of sea floor. The San Jose collided with the sand flats, her stern section disintegrated and became detached from the main hull which sank another 200 yards away with its ballast stones.
DAVIS REEF Depth Range: Shallow to 80 feet Experience Level: Novice	Davis Reef is a popular outer reef on the edge of a flat shallow bank. Huge schools of fish and several resident green moray eels have made this reef famous. Another attraction adorning this reef is a statue of a Buddha that sits on a concrete block in the middle of a sand plain.

CROCKER REEF Depth Range: 40-80 feet Experience Level: Intermediate	Crocker Reef consists of an extensive collection of formations which allows divers to explore several discrete sites within one dive.
THE EAGLE Depth Range: 75-120 feet Experience Level: Advanced	A 287-foot freighter, sunk in 1985 as part of the Florida Keys Artificial Reef Association program, forms an artificial reef which has brought enjoyment to thousands of divers. The Eagle has remained generally intact, apart from eight gaping holes in her side and although the wreck rests at a depth of 110 feet, divers will begin to encounter her superstructure at 75 feet. Because of the Eagle's comparatively remote location beyond the protective confines of the reef, the state of the current will be a vitally important factor in determining the dive plan at this site.
HENS & CHICKENS REEF Depth Range: 20-22 feet Experience Level: Novice	Hens and Chickens Reef is named because of its appearance from the air. In this group of patch reefs, the coral formations radiate outwards from the center, like a mother hen surrounded by chickens. A shallow inshore site, this reef displays a remarkable proliferation of fish and corals.
ALLIGATOR REEF Depth Range: 25-30 feet Experience Level: Intermediate	The reef was named after the USS Alligator, a schooner which ran aground here in 1825 and whose remains are still visible in the open waters southeast of its famous light tower. The reef displays spurs and grooves coursing down a moderate slope as well as more isolated coral heads. It is especially noted for its size, its deep ravines and intricately patterned coral crevices.

MIDDLE KEYS-MARATHON DIVE SITES

SOMBRERO REEF Depth Range: 6-25 feet Experience Level: Novice	Marked by Sombrero Light, the beautiful Sombrero Reef features well-defined spurs or fingers of reef building corals separated by wide channels of gleaming white sand. Brilliant colors and diverse marine life along with an eight-foot high natural coral bridge known as "The Arch" make this a very popular dive site.
DELTA SHOAL Depth Range: 6-25 feet Experience Level: Novice	Another popular dive site eastward of Sombrero Light, Delta Shoal features massive coral fingers and broad expanses of sandy bottom that separate the spurs that form this reef. Two wrecks lie in this area - the Delta Shoals Barge behind the east end features typical shallow water soft corals and an abundance of fish life, perfect for snorkeling. Little evidence remains of the Ivory Coast Wreck, a sunken slave ship lost at this site in 1853.
MARATHON'S MIDDLE REEFS **COFFINS PATCH** Depth Range: 10-25 feet Experience Level: Novice	Marathon has a wide variety of prime shallow dive locations throughout their middle reefs. Most are typically no deeper than 25 feet. and all feature an abundance of fish and a variety of coral growth. A stake marks the location of Coffins Patch, by an iron pipe that extends several feet out of the water. Legend has it that this pipe is a remnant of a mariner's light structure destroyed in the horrific 1935 Labor Day hurricane. Beware—the stake is totally encrusted with fire coral!
THUNDERBOLT WRECK Depth Range: 75-120 feet Experience Level: Advanced	A 188-foot research vessel once used for studying lightning and sunk in 1986, the Thunderbolt rests upright in 120 feet of water. At 85 feet, her bow is dominated by a huge horizontal reel. Dropping over the stern of the vessel, divers can examine huge twin props. Large hatches off the main deck open into the engine compartments where it is possible to descend into the hull to 110 feet.

ADELAIDE BAKER (The "Duck Key Wreck") Depth Range: 18-29 feet Experience Level: Novice	The Adelaide Baker was built in 1863 and was 153 feet long with a beam of 35 feet and a hold of 21 feet. She was a three-masted barque. She wrecked on January 28, 1889 while bound for Savannah with a load of sawn timber. There was no loss of life. What is left of the wreck covers over 1400 feet.
PORKFISH Depth Range: 16-27 feet Experience Level: Novice	Porkfish is a nice ledge reef alongside one of the mast sections of the Adelaide Baker. In addition to schools of tropical fish, nurse sharks are frequently seen here.
CRITTER RIDGE Depth Range: 18-31 feet Experience Level: Novice	An easily-navigated, beautiful long coral ledge, Critter Ridge gets its name from the variety of marine life that can be spotted here: turtles, eels, angelfish, conchs, skates, and beautiful varieties of corals, including a small patch of pillar coral. Dolphins may visit underwater as well.
THE GAP Depth Range: 50-80 feet Experience Level: Intermediate	A drop-off reef running east to west, The Gap slopes from a depth of 50 feet at the north end to 80 feet at the south. Divers can see larger-than-average angel fish here due to the depth. There is occasionally a strong current at this site.
40-60 REEF (Also known as "Edge of Night") Depth Range: 40-60 feet Experience Level: Intermediate	40-60 Reef is a large reef patch with a sloping edge that drops from 40 to 65 feet.
DONUT Depth Range: 8-22 feet Experience Level: Novice	Donut is quite easy to explore because of its donut-like shape, which takes about 30-45 minutes for divers to circumnavigate. The site is very popular for night dives. There are many beautiful coral heads, and the best ledge to explore is on the northwest side of the reef.
SHRIMPBOAT REEF Depth Range: 35-55 feet Experience Level: Intermediate	Shrimpboat Reef is a sloping reef with scattered remains of a shrimp boat. Due to the wreckage, there are walls with a variety of fish, colorful corals and occasional dolphins.

LOWER KEYS & KEY WEST DIVE SITES

LOOE KEY REEF Depth Range: 5-35 feet Experience Level: Novice to Intermediate and Advanced	Looe Key Reef is one of the loveliest and most prolific reefs in the Keys. The frigate H.M.S. Looe accidentally ran hard aground here in 1744. Remains of the ship lie between two fingers of coral near the eastern end of the reef, although only the ballast and anchor remain visible to the trained eye. Looe Key is a designated marine sanctuary and diving at this site is exceptional because of the variety of corals, sea fans and fish species found here.
ADOLPHUS BUSCH Depth Range: maximum depth 110 feet Experience Level: Advanced	The wreck of the Adolphus Bush is located about 5 miles off-shore of Cudjoe Key and 3 miles west of Looe Key. Prior to being sunk in 1998, large holes were cut in the ship to create access for divers. Three goliath grouper are residents on this wreck and are seen on many dives. The largest of these fish weighs about 400 pounds. The ship is 210 feet long and the maximum depth is 110 feet, making it a very good site for nitrox. This is an advanced dive and those wishing to explore the ship should have an Advanced Open Water certification or plan to be accompanied by an instructor or divemaster.
CONTENT KEYS Depth Range: 8-15 feet Experience Level: Novice	Positioned on the Gulf side southwest of Marathon, Content Keys are sheltered and provide a good alternative for shallow diving on a windy day. Rounded starlet corals grow here and numerous potholes and cracks in the coral rock make this an ideal home for both lobster and stone crab.
SOUTH BEACH PATCHES Depth Range: 15 feet Experience Level: Novice to Intermediate	South Beach Patches are small and reefs that run along the southern shore of Key West. The most prominent ones are off the foot of Duval Street, Simonton Street, Casa Marina Hotel, Bertha Street, main bathing beach and off the airport. Almost any fish life that you might normally find on the outside reef can be found here.

KEY WEST HARBOR Depth Range: 30 feet Experience Level: Advanced	Watch for heavy commercial boat traffic in Key West Harbor, which has been in use since the middle of the 16th century. At the north end of Simonton Street is a public boat ramp and dingy landing area that gives access to this advanced diving area. Interesting artifacts have been found in this location.
SAND KEY Depth Range: Awash to 3-65 feet Experience Level: All Levels	Probably the most popular dive and snorkeling spots in the Lower Keys, Sand Key is a small, unvegetated island made from ground-up coral and small shell fragments. The island is topped by a red iron lighthouse which was built in 1853 and is on the historical register. The reef itself consists mostly of rock fingers and gullies with sandy bottoms between cliff-like structures and extensive areas of staghorn and elkhorn coral.
OUTSIDE REEFS Depth Range: 40-210 feet Experience Level: Intermediate and Advanced	For the more experienced diver, all along the Keys south of the main shallow reefs, are the Gulf Stream reefs. Outside Reefs contain a prolific gallery of deep-water corals and fish, making these deep dives different from anything anywhere else in the Keys.
ROCK KEY AND EASTERN DRY ROCKS Depth Range: 5-35 feet Experience Level: All levels	Rock Key and Eastern Dry Rocks are two popular dive spots that are typical of most reef formations in the area—long fingers of coral, with sand and coral-filled canyons in between. Their real claim to fame are their 19th century wrecks which have provided huge quantities of ballast and artifacts.
WESTERN DRY ROCKS Depth Range: 5-120 feet Experience Level: Novice to Advanced	Farther away from popular reefs closer to Key West, Western Dry Rocks have not suffered the reef damage associated with heavy usage. Large quantities of elkhorn and staghorn coral, numerous crevices and caves, and large marine life make this well worth a long trip.
THE AQUANAUT Depth Range: 75 feet Experience Level: Intermediate to Advanced	The Aquanaut is the wreck of a 55' wooden salvage tug that sits upright in 75 feet of water on a flat sandy bottom near the edge of the Gulf Stream. The tug is intact and in nearly perfect condition and it is home to a variety of fish life. On the deck of the ship a macro lens is very useful.

JOE'S TUG Depth Range: 65 feet Experience Level: Intermediate to Advanced	A small tugboat, discovered by a local diver, Joe's Tug sits upright and is an easy swim-through. Open access to the wheel house and aft deck make this an enjoyable dive. Visibility is usually good due to its location outside of the reef and offers a great photographic location with a wide variety of corals and marine life.
COTTRELL REEF (GULF SIDE REEF) Depth Range: 3-15 feet Experience Level: Novice or Intermediate	Cottrell Reef is an excellent reef for beginning snorkelers and an alternative dive spot when the weather is bad on the Atlantic side of the Keys. Covered with gorgonians and sponges, the ledges and banks of this reef provide a wide variety of reef fish.
THE LAKES Depth Range: 5-30 feet Experience Level: All Levels	A fascinating snorkeling area, The Lakes is a series of grassy flats and banks completely encompassing a shallow lagoon protected by a string of islands and reefs directly west of Key West.
MARQUESAS KEYS Depth Range: 5-30 feet Experience Level: All Levels	Marquesas Keys are the only known atoll in the Atlantic Ocean. This circle of islands is about 3.5 miles across and 22 miles west of Key West. Like most of the lower Keys, these islands are a bird sanctuary and National Wilderness Area. Wrecks in this area attract large marine life and huge clusters of coral heads can be found off the entire southern edge of the islands in about 8-12 feet of water. Several of the islands have long, white, sandy beaches and excellent anchorages can be found.

GPS coordinates for over 60 artificial reef dive destinations, ranging from man-made structures to shipwrecks of over 100 meters, can be found at the Florida Fish and Wildlife Conservation Commission's Artificial Reef website.[8]

---

8   http://myfwc.com/CONSERVATION/Conserv_Progs_Habitat_Saltwater_AR.htm.

Céline, Fabien and Jean-Michel Cousteau prepare to dive in the Florida Keys National Marine Sanctuary. Photo credit: Carrie Vonderhaar, Ocean Futures Society.

Gray's Reef National Marine Sanctuary

Eighteen miles offshore of Darien lies a peculiar kind of reef. The shrimpers have learned to avoid it because the underwater ledges tear and rip their nets. Known as a "live hard-bottom habitat," Gray's Reef was, until about 10,000 years B.C., an extension of the shore. Today, these Pleistocene-era formations are drawing the interest of curious paleoarcheologists who, by donning scuba equipment, can explore this submerged landscape and search for hidden clues to the climate changes of Earth's past. Fragments of fossilized trees, mastodon bones and human tools are record-keepers of the planet's earlier environment and by carefully sifting the sand, investigators are finding hidden treasures like needles in a haystack. As they work patiently beneath the sea, modern dinosaurs swim alongside them—the loggerheads, giant reptiles from an even earlier epoch, frequent these spaces, too.

A variety of different types of marine life inhabit Gray's Reef. Photo credit: Greg McFall, Gray's Reef National Marine Sanctuary.

About Gray's Reef National Marine Sanctuary

Gray's Reef National Marine Sanctuary is the only protected natural area off the Georgia coast. The 17.5 square nautical miles (about 11,000 acres) of Gray's Reef is just a tiny part of the vast Atlantic Ocean off the Georgia coast, yet its value as a natural marine habitat is recognized both nationally and internationally.

Within the sanctuary there are both rocky ledges and sandy flat places. Gray's Reef is not a coral reef such as those found in the tropics. It is not built by living hard corals as tropical reefs are. Instead it is a consolidation of marine and terrestrial sediments (sand, shell and mud) that were laid down as loose aggregate between six and two million years ago. At one time, Gray's Reef was dry land.

A diver is framed by a ledge at Gray's Reef. Photo credit: Greg McFall, Gray's Reef National Marine Sanctuary.

Gray's Reef National Marine Sanctuary was named in recognition of Milton "Sam" Gray, who studied the area in the 1960s as a biological collector and curator at the University of Georgia Marine Institute on Sapelo Island, GA. The near-shore hard-bottom reef off the coast of Sapelo Island was recognized by Sam Gray in 1961 in connection with his extensive biological surveys of the ocean floor off the Georgia coast. Collections made during the surveys are under the protective supervision of the University of Georgia Natural History Museum and maintained as the "Gray's Reef Collection." In 1974, Jesse Hunt, a graduate student working under Dr. V. J. Henry was the first scientist to study the reef. He proposed the name "Gray's Reef" for this live-bottom habitat to commemorate Sam Gray's valuable contribution to the understanding of offshore habitats and marine organisms, especially those of the near-shore continental shelf of Georgia.

A school of juvenile grunts. Photo credit: Greg McFall, Gray's Reef National Marine Sanctuary.

Why a National Marine Sanctuary?

The Georgia Department of Natural Resources submitted a nomination to the Secretary of Commerce in June 1978 recommending the designation of Gray's Reef as a marine sanctuary based on its distinctive marine resources and potential sensitivity to environmental perturbation.

Gray's Reef National Marine Sanctuary was designated as the nation's fourth national marine sanctuary on January 16, 1981 for the purposes of protecting the quality of this unique and fragile ecological community; promoting scientific understanding of this live bottom ecosystem; and enhancing public awareness and wise use of this significant regional resource.

Fabien Cousteau observes a mass of sea stars on a sponge at Gray's Reef.
Photo credit: Carrie Vonderhaar, Ocean Futures Society.

Resources within the Sanctuary

HARD-BOTTOM COMMUNITY

Gray's Reef is a consolidation of marine and terrestrial sediments (sand, shell, and mud) laid down as loose aggregate between six and two million years ago. Coastal rivers draining into the Atlantic probably transported some of these sediments and currents brought others in from other areas. More of these sediments accumulated until a dramatic change began to take place on Earth during the Pleistocene Epoch, between two million and 8,000 years ago. It was during this time that the area that is now Gray's Reef was exposed land and the shoreline was as much as 80 miles east of its present location. As a result of this exposure, the sediments there became solidified into porous limestone sandstone rock. As the glacial ice melted, the water flowed back towards the sea, filling the basins back to their original levels.

An oyster toadfish sits on the sand between patches of reef.
Photo credit: Greg McFall, Gray's Reef National Marine Sanctuary.

Gray's Reef is a submerged hard-bottom (limestone) area that, as compared to surrounding areas, contains extensive but discontinuous rock outcroppings of moderate (six to ten feet) height with sandy, flat-bottomed troughs between. The series of rock ledges and sand expanses has produced a complex habitat of caves, burrows, troughs, and overhangs that provide a solid base for the abundant sessile invertebrates to attach and grow. This rocky platform with its carpet of attached organisms is known locally as a "live-bottom habitat." This topography supports an unusual assemblage of temperate and tropical marine flora and fauna. Algae and invertebrates grow on the exposed rock surfaces: dominant invertebrates include sponges, barnacles, sea fans, hard coral, sea stars, crabs, lobsters, snails, and shrimp. The reef attracts numerous species of benthic and pelagic fish, including black sea bass, snapper, grouper, and mackerel. Since Gray's Reef lies in a transition area between temperate and tropical waters, reef fish population composition changes seasonally. Loggerhead sea turtles, a threatened species, use Gray's Reef year-round for foraging and resting, and the reef is part of the only known winter calving ground for the highly endangered North Atlantic right whale.

Tropical species like this spotfin butterflyfish are sometimes found at Gray's Reef.
Photo credit: Greg McFall, Gray's Reef National Marine Sanctuary.

CULTURAL RESOURCES

Gray's Reef may have been a terrestrial environment as recently as 10,000 to 8,000 years ago. During this period, Gray's Reef was a shallow coastal environment supporting oysters, clams, and other estuarine organisms. Scientific divers have discovered fossils of extinct land-dwelling animals, such as ground sloth, mammoth, mastodons, camels, horses, and bison. These fossils may be associated with early human groups colonizing the North American continent in the late Ice Age. Many of the fossil finds are known prey species of these early hunters. One antler fragment recovered at Gray's Reef National Marine Sanctuary shows possible evidence of human use as a tool. In 2002, an Early Archaic Period projectile/spear point (8000-5000 years old) was found at the reef near the earlier discovery of the antler tool.

Key Species within the Sanctuary

A prominent oasis of life compared with the desert of soft mud surrounding it, Gray's Reef attracts turtles returning from their transatlantic journeys that come here to forage for food. As they continue to mature, their diets begin to shift from soft pelagic prey, small oceanic crustaceans and jellies, to beefy reef and estuarine invertebrates. Their very name, loggerhead, is, in fact, a reference to the large prominent jaws they use to crush clams, mussels and even horseshoe crabs. Brightly colored corals, sponges and sessile invertebrates carpet the ledges of the reef where lobsters, crabs and molluscs take up residence. The rich diversity of life is due in part to the reef's location in a unique convergence zone where warm tropical water from the south and the cooler temperate waters of the north meet, and the composition of species will change by season. Black sea bass, snapper, grouper, and mackerel make their homes here and can be recreationally fished. Giants, larger and more rare than loggerheads, journey here too—the nearly extinct North Atlantic right whale migrates to the waters of Gray's Reef National Maine Sanctuary in the winter to give birth.

Two black sea bass hover over the reef. Photo credit: Greg McFall, Gray's Reef National Marine Sanctuary.

SEA TURTLES

Sea turtles known to occur in the Gray's Reef National Maine Sanctuary include the Kemp's ridley, hawksbill, leatherback, green, and loggerhead. All these species except the loggerhead are federally listed as endangered species. The loggerhead sea turtle is the most abundant sea turtle in the region and is federally listed as a threatened species. Loggerhead sea turtles are frequently seen resting and foraging at Gray's Reef. Female loggerheads find Gray's Reef a nice place to live during the summer nesting season, laying their eggs on the beaches and then returning to the reef to eat and rest. They will do this from two to five times a season, laying about 120 eggs per nest. It is illegal to harm or harass these animals. Divers need to resist the temptation of touching or prodding a resting loggerhead; never try to hitch a ride on a sea turtle.

> Remember, all sea turtles can mistake floating plastic for food—stash your trash!

Divers remove monofilament fishing line from the reef.
Photo credit: Greg McFall, Gray's Reef National Marine Sanctuary.

Occasionally, a rare leatherback turtle will arrive on Wassaw or an even rarer Kemp's Ridley, but mostly, it's the mother loggerheads that come ashore under the cover of darkness to excavate nests and bury their clutch of eggs in the sand. Approximately 60 days later, the little hatchlings break free of their shells and burrow out from their sandy nests; the process of pipping to open the eggshell and crawling free can take up to seven days but more commonly is completed in four. Like expectant midwives, volunteers patiently mark the days off the calendar for each nest and stand by to collect data on the little ones as they scramble by in their mad dash for the sea.

From the moment they paddle into the vastness of the blue offshore, little more is known about their first stages of life—the "lost years." Gulls, fish, sharks, and other predators are waiting for them at the edge of the sea. If they survive this predatory onslaught, the young loggerheads will swim on, alternating subsurface powerstroking with surface dogpaddling and breathing for 20 to 30 hours more in order to catch a ride in the greater safety of the drifting Sargassum of the Gulf Stream.

A female loggerhead sea turtle uses her front flippers to clear away loose sand in preparation for nesting. Photo credit: Carrie Vonderhaar, Ocean Futures Society.

With the advent of satellite tracking, telemetry and genetic sampling, we are only beginning to unravel the mysteries of turtle migrations and where they go, but we may never know why. Hatchlings from the southeastern U.S. ride the great gyre of the North Atlantic, navigating the subtle differences in Earth's magnetic fields as waypoints on the journey to islands off Africa, then continue the ride back round again.

When the juveniles or sub-adults reappear back along the coasts of the southeastern United States, they prefer the coastal bays and estuaries of Florida, Georgia, the Carolinas, and the Gulf of Mexico to the open ocean.

A loggerhead sea turtle with large barnacles on its back.
Photo credit: Greg McFall, Gray's Reef National Marine Sanctuary.

Like so many species, the loggerheads rely on the reef for food, but the physical structure is also significant. The ledges provide escape from tiger sharks and other predators, as well as a place to doze. And crevices, concave and worn smooth, are turtle scratching posts, we've learned, after the sanctuary's Science Coordinator Greg McFall caught this rarely observed behavior on film. Gray's Reef and sea turtles share another connection, too—hitchhikers. Mike Frick noticed that incoming loggerheads at Wassaw Island arrived year after year loaded with barnacles, hydroids, crabs, sponges, and worms. Curious about these miniature gardens, he examined them more closely and found a micro version of the reef and its inhabitants (called epibionts) traveling on their carapaces. He believes turtle hosts play a substantial role in the population ecology of many crab species and, as a result, the structuring of marine habitats they both share.

A loggerhead sea turtle swims out from under a ledge.
Photo credit: Greg McFall, Gray's Reef National Marine Sanctuary.

RIGHT WHALES

It is possible to encounter a highly endangered North Atlantic right whale (sometimes referred to as the northern right whale) when visiting Gray's Reef; the Sanctuary is near the only known calving ground for the whales and near an area designated as critical habitat. Federal rules require that people get no closer to a North Atlantic right whale than 500 yards—the length of five football fields. North Atlantic right whales have been sighted from Iceland to Florida, but the only known calving area is in the coastal waters of Georgia and Florida.

The area, designated as "critical habitat," extends from the mouth of the Altamaha River in Georgia south to Sebastian Inlet, Florida, and from the shoreline out 5 to 15 miles. Peak abundance of right whales in this area, as well as calving, occurs from December through March. In March and April, right whales congregate in the plankton-rich waters of Cape Cod Bay, the Great South Channel, and Georges Bank off Massachusetts to stock up on much needed nutrients. This area has been designated the northeastern "critical habitat" for the North Atlantic right whale. These whales continue their northward travels to breeding and feeding grounds in the Bay of Fundy and off the southeastern coast of Nova Scotia where they spend the summer and fall.

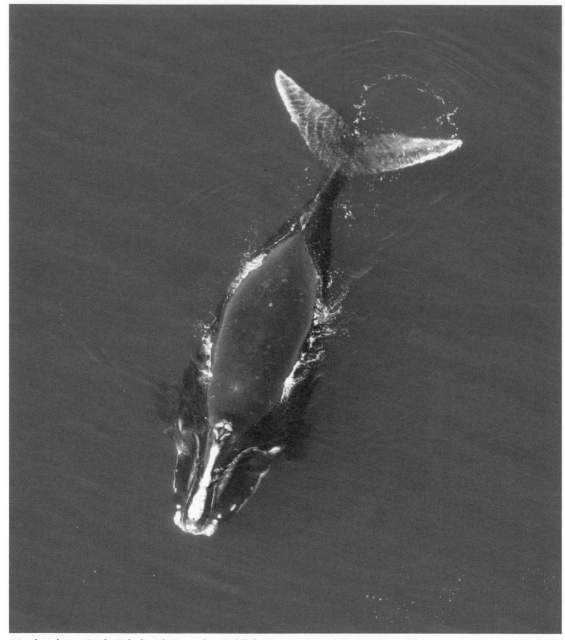

North Atlantic Right Whale. Photo credit: Wildlife Trust.

North Atlantic right whales are black with variable gray or white patches on their throats and bellies. Identifying features include the absence of a dorsal fin, a deeply notched tail with a smooth trailing edge, a large head (more than one-quarter of the body length), a narrow upper jaw and curved lower jaw. Blowholes of right whales are divided on the surface, forming two holes typical of baleen whales (toothed whales have a single blowhole). Visible from a distance, the blow is identified by a nearly vertical "V" shape. When viewed from the side or affected by wind, however, this double blow may appear as one. The right whale's flippers are short and very broad. Tough skin patches, called callosities, are used with other markings to identify individuals. Callosities are located on the top of the head, above the eye, behind the blowholes, and along the lower jaw. These areas of callused skin begin to develop soon after birth and are observed on very young right whales. Callosities appear white in color because they are colonized by small white crustaceans called cyamids. Sparse hair appears in the tips of the whale's chin and upper jaw, often associated with callosities. Large amounts of blubber, about two-fifths its body weight, give the right whale a particularly rotund appearance. Adult whales which average 40-55 feet (12-16.5 meters), can weigh almost 140,000 pounds (63.5 metric tons.)

Individual right whales can be identified by the white patches, or callosities, on their heads. Photo credit: Wildlife Trust.

Now federally protected, and the official state marine mammal for both Georgia and Massachusetts, the North Atlantic right whale was historically hunted for its commercially valuable products: oil and baleen plates. Characteristics of the right whale—a slow swimming speed, staying in close proximity to the coast and floating when dead—inspired whalers to designate this whale the "right" whale to kill.

Because North Atlantic right whales swim slowly, spending a considerable amount of time at the surface to skim feed and rest, they are susceptible to collision with vessels. Although data on the effects of vessel disturbance are not conclusive, cows with calves appear to be sensitive to sound, and have been observed avoiding boats. Unfortunately, these whales move slowly and are often unable to avoid collisions.

Although collisions with ships remain a constant threat, entanglement in derelict fishing gear is an ever-present hazard. A whale disentanglement team, led by the Center for Coastal Studies in Provincetown, Massachusetts, has successfully freed several North Atlantic right whales over the years.

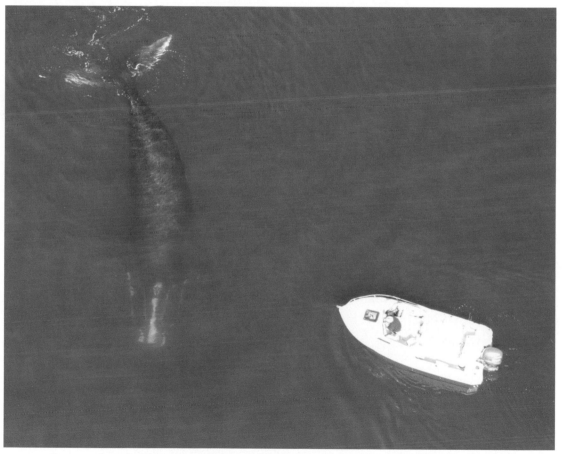

Boats need to stay 500 yards away from right whales—this boat is too close. Photo credit: Wildlife Trust.

Since 1980, a team of scientists from a consortium of research centers has surveyed the North Atlantic right whale population to determine how the whales use their habitats and whether other critical areas exist. To track the whales, researchers had to first learn how to identify and recognize individuals. Such information helps scientists determine whether individual whales return to the same areas every year, which females have given birth, how whales are related to each other, and which ones may have died. Fortunately, right whales are easy to tell apart. All whales have unique patterns of callosities on their heads. Many whales also have distinctive scars from encounters with boats. Since 1980, researchers have traveled out to some of the major habitats to photograph the whales. Then they compare the pictures to a comprehensive catalog of right whale photographs housed at the New England Aquarium. The catalog contains photos dating back to 1935, but most of the records were gathered since 1979. Few previously unidentified adult whales have been photographed in recent years, leading researchers to conclude that they have records of most of the whales in the population.

By logging the location of individuals over the course of a year, scientists have outlined a general migration route. During the winter, pregnant females travel to their calving ground to give birth. This area is so broad that despite extensive aerial surveys, researchers often miss newborns. One of the biggest mysteries, however, is where the males and non-pregnant females go during the winter. At this point, nobody knows.

In addition to the North Atlantic right whale, 21 species of whales are known to occur near Gray's Reef. These include bottlenose dolphins, spotted dolphin, humpback whales, and Bryde's whales.

To report a whale sighting or to report an injured or distressed whale, dolphin or sea turtle, call the Georgia Department of Natural Resources at 1-800-272-8363.

Young right whales often travel to the calving grounds. Their playful behavior distinguishes them from the pregnant females and new mothers. Photo credit: Wildlife Trust.

Research within the Sanctuary

Scientists study many things at Gray's Reef, including the following:

- Benthic ecology – Researchers are studying benthic invertebrates such as sponges and corals to learn how they are influenced by biological, chemical and physical factors.

- Geological mapping – Using techniques such as multibeam and sidescan sonar, and sediment coring, scientists can study the sanctuary's sea floor and look for changes caused by erosion or sedimentation.

- Fish ecology – Fish populations are studied using various methods, including acoustic technology, tagging and diver-based surveys. Current research topics include fish population genetics, predator-prey interactions, movement of fish within the sanctuary, and non-native invasive lionfish. Gray's Reef has an online reporting form for non-native lionfish sightings.[1]

- Archeology/paleontology – Researchers working at Gray's Reef discovered bones from an extinct Atlantic Gray Whale, dated to 36,000 years BP.

- Climate change – Scientists are studying potential impacts of ocean acidification, as well as air-sea carbon dioxide exchange in an attempt to determine the effects of increased atmospheric carbon dioxide on the reef.

---

1   http://graysreef.noaa.gov/pdfs/lionfish_form.pdf.

Researchers use video to record fish and invertebrates on the reef.
Photo credit: Greg McFall, Gray's Reef National Marine Sanctuary.

The Research Vessel Sam Gray.
Photo credit: Carrie Vonderhaar, Ocean Futures Society.

Visiting the Sanctuary

Note: In the last section of the book, "When You Visit the Sanctuaries," is detailed information about resources found within each sanctuary to help visitors have an enjoyable and productive visit.

ADMINISTRATIVE OFFICE

10 Ocean Science Circle
Savannah, GA 31411
Telephone: 912-598-2345

While Gray's Reef National Marine Sanctuary does not have its own visitor's center, it has exhibit partnerships with The Georgia Aquarium (Atlanta, GA), Tybee Island Marine Science Center (Tybee Island, near Savannah, GA), the Fernbank Museum of Natural History (Atlanta, GA), the University of Georgia's Marine Education Center and Aquarium (MECA) (Skidaway Island, near Savannah, GA), Georgia Southern University (Statesboro, GA), and the South Carolina Aquarium (Charleston, SC). Each of these facilities hosts an exhibit about Gray's Reef, its environment, the marine life found in the Sanctuary and the Sanctuary's importance within the National Marine Sanctuary Program. Exhibits range from dioramas to tanks with live animals to interactive displays and videos. Gray's Reef continues to expand its exhibit outreach.

The Sanctuary's staff are interested in learning about sightings of marine mammals, pelagic birds, sea turtles and oceanic fish (such as ocean sunfish) within the sanctuary. A reporting form can be downloaded from the Sanctuary's website.[2]

BOATING

The Sanctuary is only accessible by boat, and does not run boat tours, fishing trips or dive trips. However, many independent boat operators run fishing and dive trips to the

---

2   http://graysreef.noaa.gov/pdfs/wildlife_reporting_form.pdf.

Sanctuary. Most recreational vessels that operate at Gray's Reef National Marine Sanctuary range from 20 to 40 feet in length, are motorized, use fuel, and are privately owned. The sanctuary is located 17.5 nautical miles (32 kilometers) off Sapelo Island, Georgia, between Savannah and Brunswick, and 60-70 feet below the ocean surface. Most boats cruise at speeds of 10-20 knots (or nautical miles per hour,) so a boat trip from Sapelo Island would take 1-2 hours. Anchoring is not allowed in the Sanctuary.

A data buoy at Gray's Reef. Photo credit: Greg McFall, Gray's Reef National Marine Sanctuary.

Boat ramp locations and the Sanctuary boundary coordinates can be found online.[3] It is illegal to deposit any trash in the sanctuary. Fish, fish parts, bait or chumming materials are

3   http://www.georgiawildlife.org/fishing; http://graysreef.noaa.gov/newregs.html

the only acceptable disposables. People can make a big difference by picking up plastic that they see floating in the water. Birds, fish, mammals, and sea turtles can get entangled in plastic items or mistake them for food, and may die of starvation or poisoning when plastic is in their stomachs. Plastic debris in the water can also foul propellers and clog or damage engine intake systems. Sea birds, sea turtles and marine mammals can get entangled in monofilament; fishermen should not discard fishing line in the water.

Boaters need to be on the lookout for other boats flying dive flags (a red flag with a white bar at an angle) and keep at least 100 yards away—the length of a football field. This will help ensure the safety of divers who may be in the water nearby.

FISHING

Sport fishing occurs year-round but at different levels of intensity. Fishing for pelagic species such as king mackerel is one of the most popular activities; sport fishing tournaments sponsored by private fishing clubs and marinas take place in the spring and Gray's Reef is a popular destination for participants. A Georgia fishing license is required. Information on Georgia's saltwater fishing license and regulations can be found online.[4]

---

4   http://www.georgiawildlife.org/fishing/regulations.

A well-camouflaged flounder. Photo credit: Greg McFall, Gray's Reef National Marine Sanctuary.

Fishing regulations only allow the use of rod and reel and handline within the Sanctuary. Spearfishing is not allowed, and spearfishing gear is only allowed on vessels that are passing through the Sanctuary without stopping (spearfishing gear must be kept stowed.) The regulations also prohibit anchoring, alteration of and construction/abandonment on the seabed, damage to or removal of bottom formations and other natural or cultural resources, and discharge of substances or materials.

Spiny lobster. Photo credit: Greg McFall, Gray's Reef National Marine Sanctuary.

Research projects sometimes involve tagging reef fish with external and internal acoustic tags. If the fish is alive, anglers are asked to release it. If a tagged fish is not retrieved alive, anglers are asked to return the internal tag (found in the fish's abdominal cavity.)[5]

Anglers who catch a tagged fish are asked to note the tag number (the tag will be near the dorsal fin) and report the number to 912-598-2345.

---

5   http://graysreef.noaa.gov/fish_tagging_project.html

DIVING

Because Gray's Reef is an open ocean environment, divers may encounter strong currents and occasionally low visibility. The water at Gray's Reef is 50 to 70 feet (15-21 meters) deep. Since Gray's Reef is in a temperate zone the water is colder in the winter and warmer in the summer. The temperatures range from 50° F (10°C) to 80°F (26°C). Sanctuary staff and visiting scientists regularly conduct dive operations.

A diver takes underwater video at Gray's Reef.
Photo credit: Greg McFall, Gray's Reef National Marine Sanctuary.

Gray's Reef is home to over 150 species of fish, including black sea bass, snapper, grouper, mackerel, gobies, queen angelfish, barracuda, nurse sharks, and moray eels. Some of these fish only live there part of the year, depending on the temperature of the water. These fish all feed in different parts of the reef. For example, some small fish feed in small hiding places in the reef while other larger fish feed in the waters above the reef. There are five types of sharks found at Gray's Reef. They are the nurse shark, spiny dogfish, lemon shark, tiger shark and great hammerhead. Gray's Reef is also home to many types of invertebrates, including corals, comb jellies, sea anemones, sea stars, crabs, lobsters, squid, octopus, and snails.

Fabien Cousteau checks out a delicate jelly above the reef. Photo credit: Carrie Vonderhaar, Ocean Futures Society.

A school of small fish swims above brightly-colored sponges.
Photo credit: Greg McFall, Gray's Reef National Marine Sanctuary.

Close-up view of a squid. Photo credit: Greg McFall, Gray's Reef National Marine Sanctuary.

Flower Garden Banks National Marine Sanctuary

"I wasn't expecting much and instead we found such a beautiful coral reef in the middle of the Gulf of Mexico, relatively well tucked away among oil platforms and not too far away from the Dead Zone of the Mississippi coast."
— *Fabien Cousteau*

Hard-corals provide many hiding places for small fish like these blue-headed wrasses and blue chromis. Photo credit: G.P. Schmahl, Flower Garden Banks National Marine Sanctuary.

Coral reefs have declined dramatically throughout the world in the past three decades. The Global Reef Monitoring Network has estimated that 20 percent of coral reefs have been destroyed. The same report also predicts, ". . . that 24 percent of the world's reefs are under imminent risk of collapse through human pressures; and a further 26 percent are under a longer term threat of collapse." When corals die, their exposed skeletons are quickly colonized by algae leaving a severely impacted ecosystem. Loss of the corals sparks a chain reaction of death in which many of the reef's inhabitants also meet their demise as the structure of the ecological community unravels.

The Flower Garden Banks are very old compared with many Caribbean reefs. Dr. Mark Vermeij, a coral reef researcher at the University of Hawaii explains, "It took an extremely long time for these species with growth rates of less than half-an-inch per year to achieve the size they are today. These reefs are therefore probably what reefs used to look like throughout the Caribbean before their exponential decline started in the early '80s. Not only are the Flower Garden Banks unique in the present, they also provide a window to the past and a baseline that can be used to restore reefs elsewhere."

About Flower Garden Banks National Marine Sanctuary

Picture yourself over 100 miles from land, in the middle of the Gulf of Mexico. At times, the seas can be very unforgiving, and the weather can turn foul in an instant. But here, in the midst of this unpredictable Gulf, lie three of the most beautiful and wild places in the entire world. Manta rays, whale sharks, coral heads bigger than cars, hundreds of species of fish and invertebrates... this place teems with life! The Flower Garden Banks National Marine Sanctuary, located about 115 miles off the coasts of Texas and Louisiana, harbors the northernmost coral reefs in the continental United States and serves as a regional reservoir of shallow water Caribbean reef fishes and invertebrates. The coral reefs rise to within 55 feet of the surface and form the basis for a complex, yet balanced ecosystem. The Banks themselves are surface expressions of salt domes whose formation began 160 to 170 million years ago in what was a shallow sea, subject to evaporation. Today it has become a premier diving destination and attracts scientists from around the world.

A diver swims above the Flower Garden Banks reefs.
Photo credit: E. Hickerson, Flower Garden Banks National Marine Sanctuary.

The Flower Garden Banks was designated as the 10th National Marine Sanctuary on January 17, 1992. The coral-sponge communities of Stetson Bank were added to the Sanctuary in 1996. The Flower Garden Banks is the only National Marine Sanctuary in the Gulf of Mexico. With a total area of about 56 square miles (almost 36,000 acres), the sanctuary is divided among three distinct areas: East Flower Garden Bank, West Flower Garden Bank and Stetson Bank. Miles of open ocean ranging from 200-400 feet (61-122 meters) deep separate these banks, and each bank has its own set of boundaries.

Photo credit: E. Hickerson,
Flower Garden Banks National Marine Sanctuary

Schools of chub and wrasses swim around a colony of star coral.
Photo credit: E. Hickerson, Flower Garden Banks National Marine Sanctuary.

Why a National Marine Sanctuary?

Snapper and grouper fishermen discovered the Flower Garden Banks in the late 1800s. They named the banks after the brightly colored sponges, plants, and other marine life they sometimes snagged and brought to the surface. In the late 1960s, Robert Alderdice and James Covington established the Flower Gardens Ocean Research center (FGORC), heralding a period of intense multi-agency, interdisciplinary research, which continues to this day. Results of this on-going research prompted government agencies to begin discussing the need to protect the banks from increasing human activities, including oil and gas extraction, anchoring on the reefs and harvesting fish, corals and other invertebrates. With passage of the Marine Research and Sanctuaries Act in 1972, researchers began discussing the Flower Garden Banks as a candidate for designation as a National Marine Sanctuary. Twenty years later, Flower Gardens Banks became the nation's tenth National Marine Sanctuary.

"Very early on," Sanctuary Manager G.P. Schmahl explains, "we realized that if we wanted to make a sanctuary work in the Gulf of Mexico, we had to establish a relationship with the oil and gas industry and we had to be able to co-exist . . . or it would never be successful."

Gas platform High Island 389A in Flower Garden Banks National Marine Sanctuary.
Photo credit: Carrie Vonderhaar, Ocean Futures Society.

But it's an ideal based on more than just verbal handshakes. The research efforts at the Flower Garden Banks National Marine Sanctuary have been crucial to assessing the truth behind it. A coral reef monitoring project established here in 1978 is one of the longest running programs anywhere in the world. And what it has shown is that the Flower Gardens are some of the ocean's healthiest reefs in spite of the proximity of the natural gas platform that operates within a mile of it. "So this is successful and we try to let people know that such types of activities can occur in close proximity to sensitive natural features if they are operated correctly," says Schmahl.

Resources within the Sanctuary

SALT DOMES

Located about 115 miles directly south of the Texas/Louisiana border, East and West Flower Garden Banks are actually salt domes rising above the sea floor. Stetson Bank, located about 30 miles northwest of West Flower Garden Bank, is also a salt dome formation. What is a salt dome? To understand, we have to go back in history about 160 to 170 million years, when the Gulf of Mexico was a very shallow sea. The hot dry climate at that time caused a lot of evaporation, depositing layers of salt on the sea floor. As the Gulf of Mexico deepened and rivers began to flow from the land to the sea, sediments were steadily deposited over the salt layers. Eventually, internal pressures became great enough that the salt layers began to push against the overlying sediments, forcing the seafloor to bulge upward in distinct domes.

Salt domes occur across the continental shelf of the northwestern Gulf of Mexico. Some salt domes even occur on land in coastal Louisiana and Texas. High Island, TX and Avery Island, LA are two examples.

CORAL REEFS

The Flower Garden Banks National Marine Sanctuary encompasses a variety of habitat types, including the northernmost coral reefs in the continental United States. The Flower Gardens coral reef community probably began developing on top of the salt domes 10,000 to 15,000 years ago. The community has thrived sufficiently to obscure all trace of the deformed bedrock on which it developed, replacing it with dense coral reefs.

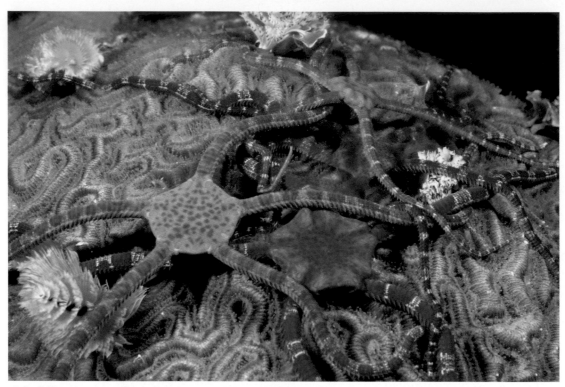

Colorful brittle stars and Christmas-tree worms on a brain coral.
Photo credit: G.P. Schmahl, Flower Garden Banks National Marine Sanctuary.

The nearest tropical reefs to the Flower Gardens are 400 miles away off the coast of Tampico, Mexico. Scientists believe that corals at the Flower Gardens probably originated from Mexican reefs when currents in the western Gulf of Mexico carried the young corals (planulae), other animal larvae, and plant spores northward. A few of these planulae were lucky enough to settle on the hard substrate of the Flower Gardens.

Amazingly, this location in the northwestern Gulf provided all the comforts of home for hard corals: a hard surface for attachment, clear sunlit water, warm water temperatures (between 68 and 85 degrees Fahrenheit), and a steady food supply. The corals now form the basis for a complex, yet balanced ecosystem, providing a regional oasis for shallow-water Caribbean reef species.

Schools of fish swim over the reef. Photo credit: G.P. Schmahl, Flower Garden Banks National Marine Sanctuary.

Stetson Bank is located about 30 miles northwest of the West Flower Garden Bank. That small difference in location produces an amazing difference in the habitat. Because of their more northerly position, the winter water temperatures are four degrees cooler, on average, than the Flower Garden Banks. That small temperature difference is enough to prevent corals from growing fast enough to develop into a coral reef, as they have at the Flower Garden Banks. Instead, there are individual coral colonies interspersed with a much denser population of sponges. The siltstone bedrock shows through in many places.

Silhouette of a diver at Stetson Bank, located about 48 km northwest of the Flower Garden Banks. The coral-sponge communities of Stetson Bank were added to Flower Garden Banks National Marine Sanctuary in 1996. Photo credit: G.P. Schmahl, Flower Garden Banks National Marine Sanctuary.

While the predominant coral species at the Flower Gardens are large boulder shaped corals such as brain coral and mountainous star coral, the prevalent species at Stetson are smaller encrusting corals, such as fire coral and green cactus coral. Divers describe the effect as an underwater moonscape.

Beginning to descend through the water column into this unspoiled wilderness, divers will pass through the pelagic zone. Here are those species that survive by cruising from place to place in search of a meal or a mate. These include such charismatic characters as manta and spotted eagle rays, hammerhead and silky sharks, the ubiquitous chub, loggerhead sea turtles, jack crevalle, amberjack, and, just possibly, a whale shark.

A spotted moray eel peeking out from under some coral in Flower Garden Banks National Marine Sanctuary.
Photo credit: G.P. Schmahl, Flower Garden Banks National Marine Sanctuary.

Just below 50 feet on the Flower Garden Banks is the reef cap, which continues to depths around 120-140 feet. The more than 300 acres of marvelous high relief reefs include the majority of the species found at the Flower Gardens: about 23 species of corals, over 250 reef invertebrate species, more than 175 types of fish, and over 80 species of marine algae. Until recently, it was thought that the Flower Garden Banks had no large branching coral species, such as elkhorn or staghorn coral. Nor were the banks thought to be home to more than a sprinkling of "soft corals" such as sea whips or sea fans. Explorations in recent years, however, have revealed at least two colonies of elkhorn coral. Improved underwater camera and video technology, combined with access to high-resolution sonar data and remotely operated vehicles have been key to documenting many additional species of "soft corals" such as gorgonians.

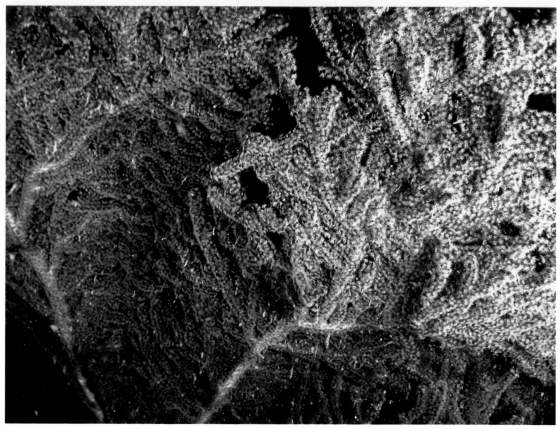

Muricea pendula is one of many gorgonians living in deeper areas around Flower Garden Banks National Marine Sanctuary. This image was taken using a Remotely Operated Vehicle (ROV). Photo credit: FGBNMS/NURC-UNCW.

The most obvious organisms found on the reef cap are the massive boulder-shaped coral colonies. Many have been sculpted into mushroom shapes by a process called bioerosion, in which other organisms gradually wear away the colony around its base. Available space created by bioerosion and breakage is quickly colonized by algae, sponges, and other attaching organisms. The dominant coral species are mountainous star corals and brain coral.

Erosion of the limestone rock at the base of the coral colonies results in their mushroom-like shape.
Photo credit: G.P. Schmahl, Flower Garden Banks National Marine Sanctuary.

Below 90 feet on the reef cap are, nestled among the larger corals, ridges or knolls with high concentrations of a small branching finger coral. These unusual thickets also feature finger sponges, encrusting sponges and algae. The finger coral ridges are also found scattered around the deeper reef habitat.

A thriving field of finger coral at East Flower Garden Bank in August 2005.
Photo credit: G.P. Schmahl, Flower Garden Banks National Marine Sanctuary.

To examine these habitats, divers must venture below 120 feet into water as deep as 170 feet—not advisable for the average recreational diver. At these depths, corals grow in a flattened manner to maximize their exposure to light, a critical element of life to the symbiotic algae living in the corals' tissues. Habitat relief is much lower than on the shallow reefs. Fewer hard corals live in this zone, primarily because most species need more light. The dominant species are a type of star coral and fire coral.

This octopus was spotted near a sponge and solitary cup coral in deeper areas of Flower Garden Banks National Marine Sanctuary. The photo was taken using a Remotely Operated Vehicle (ROV). Photo credit: FGBNMS/NURC-UNCW.

East and West Flower Garden Banks are presently in good condition, compared to most other reef systems of the Caribbean and western Atlantic. Over 20 years of long-term coral reef monitoring at the East and West Flower Garden Banks indicates that the reefs have maintained approximately 50-70% coral coverage within the coral zone - an extraordinary coverage in a global climate of coral reef decline.

A large tube sponge. Photo credit: E. Hickerson, Flower Garden Banks National Marine Sanctuary.

ALGAL-SPONGE HABITAT

At about 150 feet, the algal-sponge habitat begins. It extends to around 270-290 feet deep. Dominated by coralline algae, this habitat covers several square miles, a much larger area than is inhabited by corals. Algal nodules, up to fist size, cover 50-80 percent of the bottom in places. Because of the area covered and the amount of carbonate deposits produced, the algae may be more important to reef formation, overall, than corals are on the banks. Although less is known of the biota in this habitat, some believe that the species diversity may be comparable to that on the reef cap.

The lower two-thirds of the algal-sponge habitat begin a transition zone between organisms that exhibit distinct shallow-water traits and those adapted to deep water. A distinctive transition species is a white, bedspring-shaped sea whip, which belongs to the black coral family.

UNDERWATER SALT LAKE

Along the southeast flank of the East Bank, at about 220 feet deep, is an unusual underwater salt lake almost 200 feet wide and only ten inches deep. Fed by a brine seep from the underlying salt dome, the lake is highly saline, has high levels of hydrogen sulfide and dissolved hydrocarbon gases, and no oxygen—not exactly what we think of as ideal living conditions for most organisms. The lake flows into a canyon that allows mixing to occur. This dilutes the brine, adds oxygen and reduces the toxic hydrogen sulfide. So much salt has dissolved from beneath the bank that a large depression, known as a graben, has formed. The graben is more than a mile across and 15 feet deep.

A unique assemblage of biota has developed in and around the lake and in the canyon. Dominant organisms are sulfide-oxidizing bacteria, living at the very thin interface between the dense brine lake and the normal sea water above. A white mat of bacteria and algae covers the floor of the canyon. A specialized community of organisms, called thiobios, inhabits the sulfide-rich canyon stream and feed directly on the plants and bacteria growing there. Most fish cannot tolerate the sulfide of the canyon brine stream, but some are able to take advantage of the food source there by diving into it for quick meals.

RELIC REEFS

Scattered throughout the deeper portions of the Banks, where coralline algae do not thrive and reef-building corals are totally absent, are remnants of ancient reefs. These drowned reefs are the remains of habitats that probably formed during periods of lower sea levels when they were closer to the surface. Now, the depths and comparatively turbid conditions limit the species diversity. Until recently, it was believed that the areas surrounding the base of the banks were quite flat and mostly unvegetated sand or mud bottom. Improved mapping technology has revealed that these areas are much more complex than previously thought. They may actually form a sort of "fish highway" between banks, providing protection from predators and sources of food for animals moving between the banks. Even the sandy areas are more diverse than many people imagine. They support healthy communities of organisms living on and within the sediments. Microalgae, a variety of worm species, crabs and sea stars are examples of the organisms inhabiting these areas.

OIL AND GAS PLATFORMS

In the Gulf of Mexico are thousands of oil and gas production platforms that serve as de-facto artificial reefs by providing a hard surface to which larvae and spores may attach themselves. Scientists are still assessing the extent to which this system of platforms affects the overall biological productivity of the Gulf.

A large tube sponge in front of the supporting structure for an oil or gas platform.
Photo credit: Carrie Vonderhaar, Ocean Futures Society.

In front of us looms High Island 389A, one of 3,000 gas and oil platforms operating in the offshore waters of the Gulf of Mexico. We've steamed past dozens already, but 389A is unique among the thousands of steel high-rises that spring out of the sea; it is the only commercial gas platform within the boundaries of the Flower Garden Banks National Marine Sanctuary. She towers above us by eight stories and the Holo Kai's Captain, Mike Janovsky, radios the crew of the platform for permission to cast a line and tie up. Our plan is to investigate the real estate beneath the waterline and the tales we've heard of the fantastic diversity of life that takes up residence around these rigs. Peering beneath the surface, the structure slips into the abyss; the bottom lies far below, somewhere near 400 feet.

The structure of the platforms can provide refuge for many species of fish.
Photo credit: Carrie Vonderhaar, Ocean Futures Society.

Under water, the angular geometry crisscrossing around us is softened by the growth of organic life that covers every inch of the massive legs and beams that support the upper structure. Delicate hydroids, large sponges, orange cup corals, and sea fans grow everywhere. And darting all around us are snappers and grunts, some angels, and little wrasses in a frenzy. Midwater, dozens of barracudas are poised like suspended missiles ready to strike. Zim, who has worked as a commercial diver, later recalled for Jean-Michel, how clear the visibility was, saying, "It was one of the most exciting and beautiful dives off of an oil rig that I've ever encountered in my life." As we free-fall, the beams of the structure slip past us like a surrealistic glass elevator ride to the bottom of the sea. Antoine pauses the camera, Fabien is distracted and pointing below. Something large is swimming towards them. Giant pelagics—silky sharks, mantas and whale sharks—haunt these rigs and the waters around them. The dark silhouette grows larger and closer, taking the form of a sea turtle. It's a loggerhead coming up to investigate the intruders. She swims a circle around us, then, because we are noisy, boring or both, chooses not to stay, diving again towards the depths, not even surfacing for a breath.

A loggerhead sea turtle swims among the supports of a gas platform.
Photo credit: Carrie Vonderhaar, Ocean Futures Society.

CONNECTIVITY

The Flower Garden and Stetson Banks are only three among dozens of banks scattered throughout the northern Gulf of Mexico, along the continental shelf. All of these banks are part of a regional ecosystem, heavily influenced by current patterns within the Gulf. Inflows from the large watershed that drains two-thirds of the continental United States also play a significant role in the health of this region.

Currents

From the south, a current of warm water feeds the Gulf of Mexico from the Caribbean. This current enters the Gulf between Mexico's Yucatan Peninsula and Cuba. The deeper water flows up the middle of the sea, forming the Gulf Loop Current, which curves east and south along Florida's coast and exits through the Straits of Florida. The Gulf Loop is variable, sometimes barely entering the Gulf before turning; at other times, it travels almost to Louisiana's coast before swinging toward Florida. When that happens, the main current passes directly over the eastern banks along the continental shelf. Simultaneously, bits of the loop often break away from the main current and form circular eddies that move westward, across the Flower Garden, Stetson and other banks to the west. This influx of water brings with it animal larvae, plant spores and other imports from the south; it accounts for the many Caribbean species found in the northern Gulf of Mexico. During its progress, the main current is also picking up the same sorts of 'passengers' from the northern Gulf to deliver along its route back to the Caribbean and Atlantic.

Meanwhile, the shallower parts of the water flowing into the Gulf travel northwestward following the Mexico and Texas coastlines before turning east. These wind-driven currents cross over the Flower Garden, Stetson and other banks from the opposite direction of the Gulf Loop eddies and add to the Caribbean influence in the region.

Watershed

Water from 31 states flows into the Gulf of Mexico. That is more than the combined number of states whose water flows into the Atlantic and Pacific Oceans. From the north, multiple rivers drain the interior of North America into the Gulf of Mexico. The most significant of these is the Mississippi River. These rivers bring with them all of the runoff accumulated from cities, suburbs, rural areas and wildlands along their routes. Before it reaches the Gulf, this replenishing source of water is partially depleted by extractions for municipal, industrial and agricultural consumption, thus reducing freshwater inflows that sustain the estuaries. When healthy, the estuaries filter sediments and pollutants from the water, export organic material for the food chain in nearshore areas, and provide nursery areas for many species, some of which later move offshore to the system of banks along the continental shelf.

Key Species Within the Sanctuary

While everything at Flower Garden Banks National Marine Sanctuary is pretty amazing, there are some events that truly stand out. Since scientists are still learning about many of these animals and their behaviors, visitors who happen to see any are asked to please report their observations to the sanctuary office. The sanctuary staff would also love to see any photographs taken of unusual animals or events; however, boaters and divers should keep personal safety, as well as safety of the animals in mind when trying to take photographs.

Nurse shark. Photo credit: E. Hickerson, Flower Garden Banks National Marine Sanctuary.

CORAL SPAWNING

Every year, about 7-10 days after the full moon in August, usually between 9 p.m. and midnight, several coral species at the Flower Garden Banks sanctuary participate in a mass-spawning event. At this time, coral heads release their gametes into the water column where they can mix and fertilize, later becoming larvae that settle to the bottom and start new coral colonies. It's like an underwater snowstorm, in reverse.

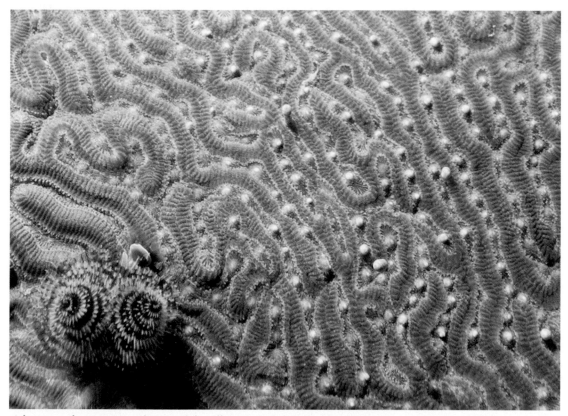

A brain coral prepares to release pink bundles containing eggs and sperm.
Photo credit: Carrie Vonderhaar, Ocean Futures Society.

Fifteen years of observations of coral spawning by scientists and diving enthusiasts around the Caribbean, the Florida Keys and here at Flower Garden Banks has contributed to a database of information about this annual event. Rarely are we so lucky to have such precise windows of predictability when it comes to the complexity of filming natural history. We pore over the charts and identification books, enthusiastically discussing the priorities for filming. Stony corals, the large massive reef builders, are actually colonies of thousands of small animals, individual polyps able to emerge and retract at will into calcium–constructed skeletons. And they can reproduce in multiple ways. One method is by asexual reproduction, where broken pieces of coral species such as the elkhorn or staghorn corals can establish new colonies. But to maintain genetic diversity, all species of corals must also undergo sexual reproduction. For an animal cemented to the seafloor, this can be a tricky process. Nature's solution is broadcast spawning, a mass synchronized event for the release of sperm and eggs into the sea. The phase of the moon and the season are the clock and calendar coral colonies around the world rely upon for the timing of their procreative jubilee. For divers seeking a firsthand experience of the spectacle, the inky darkness of the sea at night combined

Within a single species, massive coral colonies release their bundles of eggs and sperm almost simultaneously. The bundles float to the water's surface where they break open, releasing the gametes and allowing fertilization to occur. Photo credit: Carrie Vonderhaar, Ocean Futures Society.

with the weightlessness of neutral buoyancy make the experience feel closer to a journey through space than an earthly phenomena. Visually, it's like a cosmic explosion, a sensation like gliding through a galaxy littered with stardust.

"What we witnessed later was the coolest thing I've ever seen. I was in sensory overload. There was so much happening in such a short amount of time, and I knew that if I didn't capture it and soak it all in during this forty-five minute period that I would have to wait a whole year to see it again. That made this location intense. And since I had no idea what to expect, it was hard for me to mentally prepare my compositions or my exposures or decide whether to shoot macro or wide angle. That night ended up turning into this amazing wideangle shoot, a photographer's dream! Plus, I didn't expect so many and such large corals. We had just come from Key Largo where there's not very much, and then to see corals that big releasing all these eggs and sperm—I had no idea."

—*Carrie Vonderhaar*

EAGLE RAYS

Spotted eagle rays are known to school in and around the Flower Garden Banks sanctuary during the early part of the year. These rays have a pronounced head with a flat, tapered snout and a long thin tail with one to five venomous spines at the base. They have a dark back with numerous white spots and a white underside. They usually grow to about 4-7 feet (excluding tail) and like to spend most of their time between 6-80 feet in depth. Spotted eagle rays occasionally swim in pairs and sometimes even small schools. They often swim near the surface and travel long distances.

Spotted eagle ray. Photo credit: Tom Ordway, Ocean Futures Society.

HAMMERHEAD SHARKS

In the early part of the year (January through March) it is not unusual to see large schools of scalloped hammerhead sharks. Scientists don't truly know the reason for this seasonal schooling, but have noted that it is a regular occurrence in this part of the Gulf of Mexico. They have also noted that all of the sharks appear to be male. Scalloped hammerhead sharks are generally thought of as open ocean predators, although they sometimes swim through reefs and shallow areas. They are brownish-gray with a pale underside, and have an elongated head which looks like a hammer with a scalloped front edge. They hunt large fish, other sharks, rays, and invertebrates. Scalloped hammerheads grow between 5-9 feet in length and live between 20-80 feet in depth.

Socially complex, hammerhead sharks are known to congregate seasonally at predictable seamounts. Photo credit: Tom Ordway, Ocean Futures Society.

MANTA RAYS

While there is no specific time to expect manta rays at the Flower Garden Banks sanctuary, it is still an awesome experience to see one or more. These large rays glide over the reef, often swooping and turning, to capture plankton in their large open mouths. Distinctive flaps on either side of the mouth identify them as mantas, and not stingrays. So far, about 60 individual manta rays have been identified at the FGBNMS. If visitors spot a manta ray, and are able to photograph or film its underside, sanctuary staff can compare these to other images and reports. Researchers can identify individual manta rays from the characteristic spot patterns on their bellies. Research has already shown that there is a resident population of mantas, but scientists are now attaching acoustic tags to various mantas to learn more about their ranges and activities.

Underside of a manta ray. Note the spot pattern which can be used to identify individual rays.
Photo credit: Tom Ordway, Ocean Futures Society.

Atlantic manta rays are the largest species of ray in the world. They use the distinctive extensions on either side of their broad mouth to help them direct large amounts of plankton towards their mouths. Their back is typically dark brownish-black with white undersides that show dark markings. They can have "wingspans" up to 29 feet and can weigh up to 3000 pounds. Atlantic manta rays are found throughout the world and can sometimes be seen congregating in groups of up to 50 individuals where there are large concentrations of zooplankton.

A manta ray glides through the water.
Photo credit: E. Hickerson, Flower Garden Banks National Marine Sanctuary.

SEA HARES

Most people have never even heard of sea hares, but they are unusual-looking animals, and what they do in groups is, well, a bit peculiar. In June 2006, sanctuary researchers noted large numbers of sea hares at Stetson Bank. Sometimes these large, shell-less snails would swim around, using their mantle skin flaps like wings. At other times, groups of sea hares would lie on the bottom and form unique "chains" of animals, which is apparently a mating behavior. Sea hares are herbivorous, and when threatened, they may release a cloud of purple "ink" into the water.

A sea hare swimming at Stetson Bank.
Photo credit: E. Hickerson, Flower Garden Banks National Marine Sanctuary.

SQUID AGGREGATIONS

In August and September, visitors might see small squid in large groups hidden among the coral spawn, just above the reef and up in the water column. These are the elusive Roper's inshore squid (*Loligo roperi*), which form mating aggregations over the Flower Garden Banks. Though it is unclear why these squid aggregate over the banks during coral spawning, there are several possibilities. Squid might be feeding on coral spawn, which has a high fat content and is a burst of nutrition for a lot of reef dwelling animals, or they could be using the spawn as "cover" to hide from predators while conducting their own spawning, or mating, behavior. Both juveniles and adults make up these aggregations, which means not all the squid are mating. This only adds to the mystery behind the purpose of these aggregations.

WHALE SHARKS

Whale sharks are grayish-brown with white spots and lines, and a white underside. Individuals are usually between 20 and 55 feet long making them the largest fish in the world. They are filter feeders that ingest plankton, fish, squids, and pelagic crustaceans as they open their very large mouths. Whale sharks are usually seen in open water, but occasionally spend time off of coral walls and steep slopes. They are found worldwide in tropical waters at depths to 100 feet. Whale shark sightings are never "common" at the sanctuary, but they are definitely not out of the question, especially during July, August and September. Whale sharks seem to prefer the calmer surface conditions typical of that time of year as they cruise along gulping great quantities of plankton.

Whale shark. Photo credit: G.P. Schmahl, Flower Garden Banks National Marine Sanctuary.

Scientists are using acoustic tags to learn more about the whale sharks' ranges and activities. If Sanctuary visitors are lucky enough to see and photograph a whale shark, Sanctuary staff can use the spot patterns behind the gills and the first dorsal fin to help identify the individual animals. They are keen to find out whether these animals are the same ones visiting other Caribbean areas such as Belize and Mexico. A whale shark that was tagged off the Yucatan Peninsula in Mexico has visited Bright Bank in the northwestern Gulf of Mexico (about 14 miles from East Flower Garden Bank.) This confirms some level of biological connectivity between the northern and southern parts of the Gulf.

Emerging Environmental Issues

CIGUATERA

On February 5, 2008 the FDA issued a letter of guidance regarding fish caught near the Flower Garden Banks National Marine Sanctuary. The letter warns that several fish species found here may contain ciguatera toxin, which can be harmful to humans. Ciguatera toxin is produced by some species of marine algae in sub-tropical and tropical coral reef areas. When fish and invertebrates eat these algae, the toxins bioaccumulate up the food chain. This means that larger, top predatory fish can contain very high levels of ciguatera toxin in their flesh. While this does not harm the fish, ciguatera toxin can cause gastrointestinal and neurological problems in people who eat affected fish.

Fish to be avoided include the following:

<u>Within 10 miles of the Sanctuary</u>: marbled grouper, hogfish, blackfin snapper, dog snapper, gag grouper, scamp grouper, and yellowfin grouper.

<u>Within 50 miles of the Sanctuary</u>: yellow jack, horse-eye jack, black jack, king mackerel, amberjack, and barracuda.

Over 600 miles of coastal area and it inhabitants were oiled during the 2010 Gulf Oil Spill.
Photo credit: Carrie Vonderhaar, Ocean Futures Society.

OIL SPILL

In April 2010 the *Deepwater Horizon* oil well explosion began the release of what would become millions of barrels of oil into the Gulf of Mexico. Now acknowledged as the largest oil spill in the history of the United States, the potential impact on the Gulf, and the Sanctuaries located there, is unknown at this time. Jean-Michel Cousteau and his Ocean Futures Society team visited the affected areas of the Gulf on two occasions, and were the first to dive the oil and dispersant-saturated waters to document the tragedy with vivid photographs and video.

Research within the Sanctuary

Recent research in the Sanctuary includes:

- Deepwater Habitat Characterization—Historically, research at the sanctuary has focused on the coral reef caps, which account for only 1 percent of the entire sanctuary and are easily accessible with scuba equipment. More recent efforts have focused on deepwater exploration (below 170 feet), using multibeam side-scan sonar, submersibles and remotely-operated vehicles. These surveys enable researchers to better understand the biodiversity, habitats, resources and ecological processes impacting the sanctuary environment.
- Whale Shark and Manta Ray Tagging—The sanctuary has been working with the Wildlife Conservation Society to track and tag whale sharks and manta rays in the sanctuary using acoustic tags.
- Conch Tagging—This research assesses populations, establishes ranges and identifies the life-history stages of queen conch within the sanctuary.
- Long-Term Monitoring—In 1972, concerns about oil and gas production in the Gulf of Mexico prompted monitoring studies of the coral reef habitats at the East and West Flower Garden Banks, which continue to this day. Similar studies were initiated at Stetson Bank in 1993.

A close-up look at the eye stalks of a queen conch.
Photo credit: Tom Ordway, Ocean Futures Society.

The research vessel Manta is used for research, monitoring, education,
and outreach in Flower Garden Banks National Marine Sanctuary.
Photo credit: S. Du Puy, Flower Garden Banks National Marine Sanctuary.

Visiting the Sanctuary

Note: In the last section of the book, "When You Visit the Sanctuaries," is detailed information about resources found within each sanctuary to help visitors have an enjoyable and productive visit.

Flower Garden Banks National Marine Sanctuary does not have a visitor's center.

The Sanctuary's office address is:
Flower Garden Banks National Marine Sanctuary
4700 Avenue U, Building 216
Galveston, TX 77551
Phone: 409-621-5151

BOATING

There are several commercial dive and fishing charter operators that take people out to the Flower Garden Banks National Marine Sanctuary and the surrounding oil and gas platforms. Expect a three to eight hour boat ride, depending on the port of origin. The Flower Garden Banks National Marine Sanctuary was designated as a "No Anchoring Area" by the International Maritime Organization in 2001. However, vessels of 100 feet or less may tie up to the existing mooring buoys within the sanctuary on a first come, first served basis. No permit is needed to use the mooring buoys within the Flower Garden Banks National Marine Sanctuary. Mooring buoy locations and Sanctuary coordinates can be found online.[1]

---

1   http://flowergarden.noaa.gov/visiting/trip_prep.html#boundaries

Frank and Joyce Burek

Mooring buoy being installed.
Photo credit: Frank & Joyce Burek, Flower Garden Banks National Marine Sanctuary.

No matter how you choose to get to Flower Garden Banks National Marine Sanctuary, your trip will require preparation. Please remember to review standard safe boating procedures and check all safety gear to ensure it is in good working order. Also, be sure to review sanctuary regulations and remove any illegal fishing gear from your vessel before embarking on your trip.

Sanctuary regulations prohibit discharging or depositing any material into Sanctuary waters. Exceptions to these regulations include the following:

- fish, fish parts, chumming materials or bait used in or resulting from fishing with conventional hook and line gear in the sanctuary;
- biodegradable effluents incidental to vessel use and generated by an approved marine sanitation device;
- water generated by routine vessel operations *(e.g., cooling water, deck wash down, and graywater),* excluding oily wastes from bilge pumping;
- engine exhaust.

DIVING

The best way for certified SCUBA divers to learn about the sanctuary is to see it first hand, although this is sometimes easier said than done. Dive trips can be scheduled through one of the available dive charter operators; however, there may be a wait for the weather to cooperate.

*Two yellowmouth groupers eye one another
near a large brain coral in Flower Garden Banks National Marine Sanctuary.
Photo credit: G.P. Schmahl, Flower Garden Banks National Marine Sanctuary.*

Most dive professionals consider Flower Garden and Stetson Banks to be intermediate to advanced dive sites. While conditions can be calm and suitable for beginners, those occasions are extremely rare and totally unpredictable. More typically, divers will experience multiple currents, running in different directions and speeds at different depths. Currents may develop or disappear in the middle of the dive. Or, they may change direction and/or speed during the dive, requiring divers to swim against a current to return to their exit point. Wave height and frequency are also quite variable and can make it difficult to reboard the boat safely. Previous salt-water experience is strongly recommended before diving in the sanctuary. Over one hundred miles of water lie between the Flower Garden

Banks and the nearest medical facility. This is not the place to overestimate one's abilities and physical condition.

A diver begins the descent to Flower Garden Banks reefs.
Photo credit: E. Hickerson, Flower Garden Banks National Marine Sanctuary.

Only a small portion of the sanctuary is within the maximum recommended recreational dive depth of 130 feet (39.6 meters). About 2% of East Flower Garden Bank is within recreational dive limits. Stetson and West Flower Garden Banks each have less than 1% of their total area within those limits. The coral reef cap begins at about 55 feet (17 meters) in the Flower Garden Banks National Marine Sanctuary and continues to a depth of about 160 feet (49 meters). A variety of other habitats are found deeper than the reef cap, where depths range from 160-476 feet (145 meters) depending on the location within the sanctuary. Visibility in the sanctuary ranges from 75-150 feet, and water temperatures range from the mid-60's in the winter to 85°F in summer. The sanctuary has been ranked as a Top Ten destination in North America for visibility, health of the marine environment and big animals. Colorful coral meadows justify the Flower Gardens name, and divers share the water with reef dwellers, manta rays, loggerhead turtles, hammerhead and sometimes whale sharks.

A school of bait fish swims around a diver.
Photo credit: G.P. Schmahl, Flower Garden Banks National Marine Sanctuary.

A suggested checklist for divers planning to visit the Sanctuary can be found online.[2]

Snorkeling is an acceptable recreational activity in the Flower Garden Banks National Marine Sanctuary. Keep in mind, however, that the reef cap starts at 55 feet and goes deeper, so snorkelers probably won't be able to see much detail of the reef from the surface of the water. What they may get a good look at are barracuda, jacks, chubs, sea turtles, manta rays, and maybe even a whale shark. An occasional clump of *Sargassum* seaweed may also provide some interesting viewing if observed closely.

FISHING

Visitors to the Flower Garden Banks National Marine Sanctuary are only allowed to fish using traditional hook and line gear. This is defined in the regulations as any fishing apparatus operated aboard a vessel and composed of a single line terminated by a combination of sinkers and hooks or lures and spooled upon a reel that may be hand or electrically operated, hand-held or mounted. All other fishing within sanctuary boundaries, including spear fishing, is strictly prohibited.

---

2   http://flowergarden.noaa.gov/document_library/visiting/diverchecklist.pdf.

After exploring the Southeast National Marine Sanctuaries as Jean-Michel and his Ocean Futures team have, the importance of preserving these underwater treasures becomes increasingly evident. Major steps have been taken by the U.S. Government to instate higher ocean standards, but there remains much work ahead if we hope to protect and keep these incredible natural places for future generations. The National Marine Sanctuary System and the National Marine Sanctuary Foundation work year-round on behalf of these locales, and we hope that in making your way through the first section of this book, you can better understand and empathize with their plight.

There is so much to learn and admire by submerging oneself in some of the few relatively-untouched areas of water left on our planet, and it is our hope that the previous pages have inspired in you a feeling of awe and ownership toward these stretches—maybe even a desire to experience them for yourself.

If you would like to visit the Florida Keys, Gray's Reef or Flower Garden Banks sanctuaries, the pages ahead will help you have a most enjoyable experience.

When You Visit the Sanctuaries

Now that you know more about the Sanctuaries, perhaps you'd like to visit them. Whether you just stop by or get in the water with snorkel or SCUBA gear, we hope the information that follows will help you have the perfect experience.

While we've made every effort to include the most accurate and current information, it is possible that a phone number or other fact may have changed after we went to press. So, please check with the local sources for the latest information before you shove off for a visit.

The information is organized in the same order as in the Sanctuaries Section above: Florida Keys, Gray's Reef, and Flower Garden Banks.

Florida Keys National Marine Sanctuary

Sanctuary Offices

Headquarters
33 East Quay Road
Key West, FL 33040
Telephone: 305-809-4700
Fax: 305-293-5011
http://floridakeys.noaa.gov

Upper Region Office - Key Largo
P.O. Box 1083
Key Largo, FL 33037
Telephone: 305-852-7717
Fax: 305-853-0877

Lower Region Office - Key West
33 East Quay Road
Key West, FL 33040
Telephone: 305-292-0311
Fax: 305-292-5065

Florida Keys Eco-Discovery Center
35 East Quay Road
Key West, FL 33040
Telephone: 305-809-4700
http://eco-discovery.com

The following resources will help make your visit to the Florida Keys National Marine Sanctuary more enjoyable.

Chambers of Commerce

There are five separate chambers serving the Florida Keys. Each one has specific information about services and businesses within the geographic area it serves.

Key Largo Chamber of Commerce
106000 Overseas Highway
Key Largo, FL 33037
Telephone: 305-451-4747
Toll Free: 800-822-1088
Fax: 305-451-4726
Email: info@keylargochamber.org

Islamorada Chamber of Commerce
Mile Marker 83.2
P.O. Box 915
Islamorada, Fl 33036
Telephone: 305-664-4503
Fax: 305-664-4289
Toll Free: 800-FAB-KEYS/800-322-5397
Email: info@islamoradachamber.com

Greater Marathon Chamber of Commerce
12222 Overseas Highway
Marathon, Florida 33050
Telephone: 305-743-5417
Fax: 305-289-0183
Toll Free: 800-262-7284
E-Mail: visitus@floridakeysmarathon.com

Lower Keys Chamber of Commerce
31020 Overseas Highway, MM 31
Big Pine Key, FL 33043
Telephone: 305-872-2411
Fax: 305-872-0752
Email: info@lowerkeyschamber.com

Key West Chamber of Commerce
510 Greene St., 1st Floor
Key West, Florida 33040
Telephone: 305-294-2587
Fax: 305-294-7806
Email: info@keywestchamber.org

Map

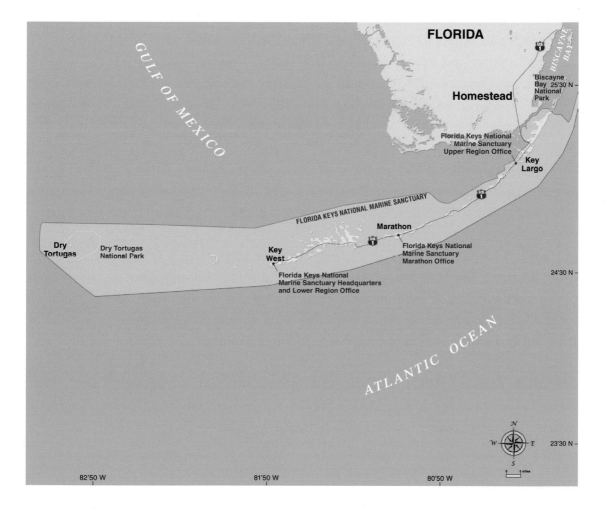

Air Transportation

Three commercial airports and one regional airport provide access by air to the Florida Keys.

For commercial flights to South Florida, **Miami International Airport** (MIA, www.miami-airport.com) and **Fort Lauderdale/Hollywood International Airport** (FLL, www.broward.org/airport) provide regular airline flights to the upper end of the Sanctuary. Both airports are served by most large airlines and several regional carriers, and a large number of car rental agencies can be found at the airports and nearby locations.

Key West International Airport (EYW, www.keywestinternationalairport.com) serves the lower end of the Keys with commercial flights from Miami International Airport and some other Florida cities. Generally, six airlines service the airport: American Eagle, Continental Airlines, Delta Connection/ComAir, United Express and US Airways.

Most flights to Key West are routed through Miami International Airport, but you can find some direct flights from major cities in Florida and the Bahamas. Several major air carriers schedule regular service to both Key West airport and Marathon airport. These include US Airways and Delta, and American Eagle Airlines.

Marathon Airport (MTH, www.fla-keys.com/marathon/marathon_airport.cfm), a regional facility, provides air access in the middle Keys to both private pilots and some commercial commuter flights.

> **Aircraft charter operators** at Marathon Airport include:
>
> Air Key West
> Telephone: 305-923-4033
>
> AirStar Executive Airways
> Telephone: 305-395-6289

Collins Aviation Air Taxi
Telephone: 305-481-3505

Gold Aviation
Telephone: 954-359-9919
Toll Free: 866-379-9106

SeaCoast Airlines
Toll Free: 866-302-6278

General Aviation Service

Two fixed base operators provide general aviation services.

Marathon General Aviation
Telephone: 305-743-4222

Marathon Jet
Telephone: 305-743-1995

Ground Transportation

Buses and Shuttles

Greyhound Keys Shuttle
Toll Free: 800-231-2222
www.greyhound.com
Daily scheduled departures from Miami and the Miami International Airport to
all areas in the Keys, ending at the Key West International Airport.

Keys Shuttle
Telephone: 305-289-9997
Toll Free: 888-765-9997
www.keysshuttle.com
Daily scheduled service throughout the Keys and to/from Miami and Fort Lauderdale.

Water Ferry

A daily ferry service is available between Key West and two cities on the southwest Florida coast, Fort Myers and Marco Island.

Key West Express
Toll Free: 888-539-2628
www.seakeywestexpress.com

Rental Car Agencies

All major car rental companies are located at **Miami, Fort Lauderdale/Hollywood**, and **Key West** airports, either directly on site or nearby, and can be found easily in telephone directories or online.

Car rental agencies located nearby the **Marathon Airport** are Avis, Budget, Enterprise, Hertz, and Thrifty.

Accommodations, Restaurants, Markets, and Attractions

Because of the wide variety of commercial enterprises available to the public, we recommend that visitors check with area Chambers of Commerce for lists of local businesses in all categories, from where to stay to where to eat and what to do.

Diving operations

Blue Star is a program established by the Florida Keys National Marine Sanctuary to reduce the impact of divers and snorkelers on the coral reef ecosystem of the Florida Keys.

It is a voluntary recognition program saluting charter boat operators who promote responsible and sustainable diving and snorkeling practices, thereby helping to keep the reef healthy for generations to come.

Blue Star recognized operators (www.sanctuaries.noaa.gov/bluestar/operators.html) are those who have dedicated themselves to leading responsible operations and providing opportunities to learn about the wonders of the sanctuary and the coral reef ecosystem. Refer to the web site for a current list of participating operators.

Blue Star operators are committed to responsible tourism and go the extra step to educate their customers about the coral reef ecosystem, the Florida Keys National Marine Sanctuary, and diving and snorkeling etiquette.

Blue Star operators at the time of publication are:

> Amy Slate's Amoray Dive Resort
> 104250 Overseas Highway
> Key Largo, Florida 33037
> Telephone: 305-451-3595
> Toll Free: 800-4-AMORAY (800-426-6729)
> Fax: 305-453-9516
> Email: amoraydive@amoray.com
> www.amoray.com/dive.html

Dive Key West
3128 N. Roosevelt Blvd.
Key West, FL 33040
Telephone 305-296-3823
Toll Free: 800-426-0707
Fax: 305-296-0609
Email: info@divekeywest.com
www.divekeywest.com

Coral Reef Park Company, Inc.
John Pennekamp Coral Reef State Park
102601 Overseas Highway (MM 102.6)
P.O. Box 1560
Key Largo, FL 33037
Telephone: 305-451-6300
E-mail: pennekamppark@yahoo.com
www.pennekamppark.com

Keys Diver and Snorkel Center
99696 Overseas Highway, Unit 1
Key Largo, Florida 33037-2432
Telephone: 305-451-1177
Toll Free 888-289-2402
E-mail:info@keysdiver.com
www.keysdiver.com

Rainbow Reef Dive Center
100800 Overseas Highway
Mile Marker 100.8
Key Largo, FL 33037
Telephone: 305-451-7171
Toll free: 800-457-4354
E-mail: divers@rainbowreef.us
www.rainbowreef.us

Fishing Guides

For those who are more into fishing than diving, the Florida Keys offer world class opportunities for heavy and light tackle enthusiasts. The following Internet sites provide a varied list of professional fishing guides and boat charters.

> www.floridakeys.com/floridakeysfishing.htm
> www.fishingfloridakeys.com
> www.fishfloridakeys.com
> www.florida-keys.fl.us/fishing.htm

Essentially, any and all types of boats are available throughout the Florida Keys and can be delivered to your dock or door. From sailboats to jet-skis to powerboats to motorboats to sailing yachts to catamarans to motor yachts and luxury yachts, the list is endless.

Boating and sailing schools (American Sailing Association standards) offer lessons, classes, charters, and clubs.

> Florida Keys Sailing (Marathon)
> www.sailfloridakeys.com

> Reef Runner Sailing (Key Largo)
> www.rrsailing.com

> Sunshine Coast Adventures (Tavernier)
> www.sunshinesailing.com

> Southernmost Sailing (Key West)
> www.southernmostsailing.com

Clean Marinas

The Florida *Clean Marina* Program is a voluntary designation program with a proactive approach to environmental stewardship. Participants receive assistance in implementing Best Management Practices through on-site and distance technical assistance, mentoring by other *Clean Marinas* and continuing education. To become designated as a *Clean Marina*, facilities must implement a set of environmental measures designed to protect Florida's waterways. These measures address critical environmental issues such as sensitive habitat, waste management, storm water control, spill prevention and emergency preparedness. Designated facilities and those facilities seeking designation receive ongoing technical support from the Florida *Clean Marina* Program and the *Clean Boating* Partnership.

A list of participating Clean Marinas is available at www.dep.state.fl.us/cleanmarina/marinas.htm#s. We recommend that you check the web site for a current list.

Remember, if you can't find what you are looking for in these pages, contact the local area Chamber of Commerce for help. Even if they don't know the answer to your question, they will find it for you. Enjoy your Sanctuary visit.

Gray's Reef National Marine Sanctuary

Sanctuary Office

The administrative offices are located on Skidaway Island near Savannah, GA., on the campus of the Skidaway Institute of Oceanography.

> 10 Ocean Science Circle
> Savannah GA 31411
> Telephone: 912-598-2439
> Fax: 912-598-2367
> www.graysreef.noaa.gov

Gray's Reef **does not** have a Visitor's Center.

A "virtual" visit to Gray's Reef, however, can be experienced at one of their exhibit partnerships. Each of these facilities hosts an exhibit about Gray's Reef, its environment, the marine life found there and its importance within the National Marine Sanctuary Program. Exhibits range from dioramas to tanks with live animals and invertebrates to interactive displays and videos.

> Georgia Aquarium, Atlanta, GA
> www.georgiaaquarium.org/exploreTheAquarium
>
> Tybee Island Marine Science Center, Tybee Island, near Savannah, GA
> www.tybeemarinescience.org
>
> The Fernbank Museum of Natural History, Atlanta, GA
> www.fernbankmuseum.org

University of Georgia's Marine Education Center and Aquarium (MECA),
Skidaway Island, near Savannah, GA
www.marex.uga.edu/aquarium/publicAquarium.html

Georgia Southern University, Statesboro, GA
www.georgiasouthern.edu

South Carolina Aquarium, Charleston, SC
www.scaquarium.org

National Aquarium, Baltimore, MD
www.aqua.org

Visiting the reef as a diver **requires experience in open-water diving**. Opportunities, therefore, for a firsthand encounter with the underwater world of the Sanctuary for novice divers is limited. The Sanctuary, however, is popular with recreational anglers, boaters and more experienced divers.

The Sanctuary **does not** run boat tours, fishing trips, or dive trips. The only way to access the Sanctuary area is by private boat, including those operated by diving or fishing charters.

The following resources will help make your visit to Gray's Reef more enjoyable.

Chamber of Commerce

Savannah Area Chamber of Commerce
101 East Bay Street
Savannah, GA 31401-1292
Telephone: 912-644-6400
www.savannahchamber.com

Map

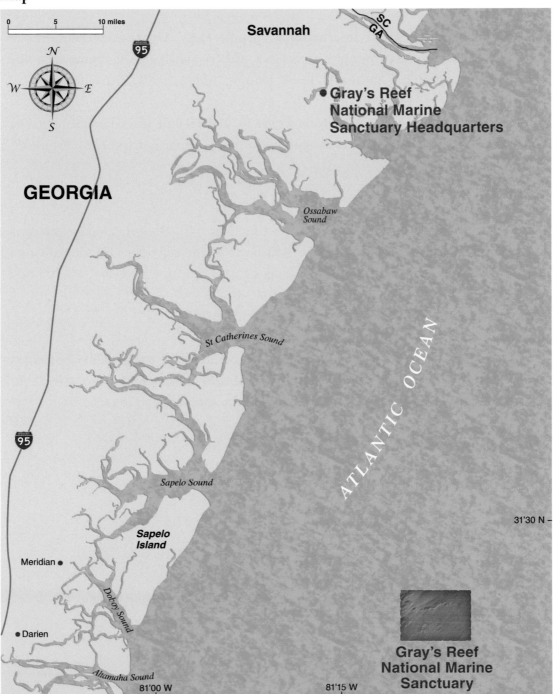

0   5   10 miles

N
W   *E*
S

Savannah

SC
GA

● Gray's Reef
National Marine
Sanctuary Headquarters

GEORGIA

95

95

*Ossabaw
Sound*

St Catherines Sound

Sapelo Sound

**Sapelo
Island**

Meridian ●

● Darien

Doboy Sound

Altamaha Sound

ATLANTIC OCEAN

31'30 N –

**Gray's Reef
National Marine
Sanctuary**

81'00 W   81'15 W

Air Transportation

The **Savannah/Hilton Head International Airport** (SAV, www.savannahairport.com) provides commercial and private aircraft access to the Savannah area. Commercial airlines include American Eagle, Continental, Delta, United Express, and US Airways.

A number of fixed base operators provide service for charter and general aviation interests. A list of companies is available at www.savannahairport.com/airport/general_aviation/.

Ground Transportation

Rental car agencies with offices at the airport include Avis, Budget, Dollar, Enterprise, Hertz, National/Alamo, and Thrifty, all of which can be located online by company name or at www.savannahchamber.com.

Accommodations, Restaurants, Markets, and Attractions

Because of the wide variety of commercial enterprises available to the public, we recommend that visitors check with Savannah Area Chamber of Commerce for lists of local businesses in all categories, from where to stay to where to eat and what to do.

Diving Operations

Dive Operators

> Divers Den Georgia
> 1050 Kings Bay Road
> St. Marys, GA 31558
> Telephone: 912-882-7078
> E-mail: diversdenstaff@yahoo.com
> www.diversdengeorgia.com

Island Dive Center
101 Marina Drive
St. Simons Island, GA 31522
Telephone: 912-638-6590
E-mail: scubadive@thebest.net

Mako Dive Charter
6 Topsail Court
Savannah, Georgia 31411
Telephone: 912-604-6256
E-mail: captwalt@makodivecharter.com
makodivecharter.com

Scubamarket USA
82-B Longwood Drive
Richmond Hill, GA 31324
Telephone: 912-756-5260
Toll Free: 888-899-9417
E-mail: sales@scubamarketusa.com
www.scubamarketusa.com

We recommend that you check the Internet or telephone directories for current listings.

Fishing guides

There are numerous charter fishing boats that go to Gray's Reef, however, a comprehensive list is not available at this time. We suggest, therefore, that the Gray's Reef Sanctuary Advisory Council representative for fishing, Capt. Wendell Harper, be contacted. He can provide additional information about local charters in the area. He may be reached at:

Capt. Wendell Harper
Free Spooling Charters
Two-Way Fish Camp
Brunswick, GA
Telephone: 912-437-8200
Mobile: 912-222-0591

Also, we recommend that you check the Internet or telephone directories for other possible listings.

Clean Marinas

The State of Georgia has implemented a clean marina program that is designed to reduce the amount of non-point source pollution in coastal Georgia counties through voluntary marine business compliance. Program goals are (1) to help marinas prevent water pollution, (2) to recognize marinas for doing so, and (3) through publicity, show boaters which marinas are participants in the program.

More information and a list of participating marinas can be found at www.uga.edu/clean-marina. We recommend that you check the web site for a list of current marinas.

Remember, if you can't find what you are looking for in these pages, contact the local area Chamber of Commerce for help. Even if they don't know the answer to your question, they will find it for you. Enjoy your Sanctuary visit.

Flower Garden Banks National Marine Sanctuary

Sanctuary Office

Flower Garden Banks National Marine Sanctuary
4700 Avenue U, Building 216
Galveston, TX 77551
Telephone: 409-621-5151
Fax: 409-621-1316
E-mail: flowergarden@noaa.gov
www.flowergarden.noaa.gov

The Sanctuary **does not** have a visitor center; however, Sanctuary displays can be viewed at the following partner sites:

Tennessee Aquarium, Chattanooga, TN
www.tennis.org

Texas State Aquarium, Corpus Christi, TX
www.texasstateaquarium.org

Audubon Aquarium - New Orleans, LA
www.auduboninstitute.org/visit/aquarium?utm_source=site

Aquarium at Moody Gardens, Galveston, TX
www.moodygardens.org

Cameron Park Zoo Aquarium, Waco, TX
www.cameronparkzoo.com

Texas Seaport Museum, Galveston, TX
www.galvestonhistory.org/Texas_Seaport_Museum.asp
(kiosk to be installed in late 2010)

Texas A&M University, Galveston, TX
www.tamug.edu
(kiosk to be installed 2010)

The Children's Aquarium at Fairpark, Dallas, TX
www.dallaszoo.com/aquarium/aquarium.htm
(exhibit to be available late 2010)

Chambers of Commerce

Galveston (TX) Chamber of Commerce
519 25th Street
Galveston, TX 77550
Telephone: 409-763-5326
Fax: 409-763-8271
www.galvestonchamber.com/index.asp

Brazosport Area (TX) Chamber of Commerce
(Serves Freeport and 7 other cities)
300 Abner Jackson Parkway
Brazosport, TX 77566
Telephone: 979-285-2501
Fax : 979-285-2505
Email: chamber2@sbcglobal
www.brazosport.org

Map

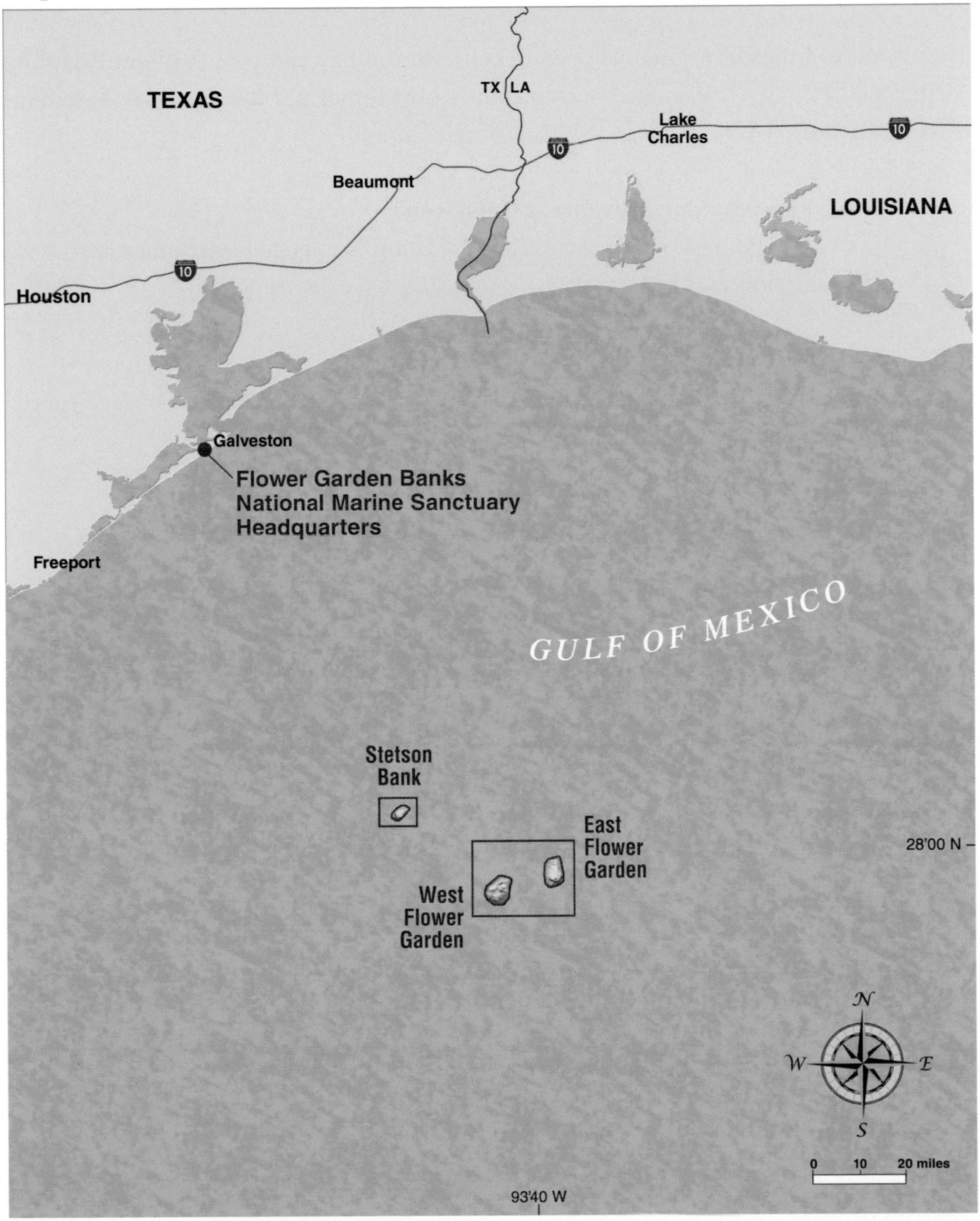

TEXAS

TX LA

Lake
Charles

Beaumont

LOUISIANA

Houston

Galveston

**Flower Garden Banks
National Marine Sanctuary
Headquarters**

Freeport

GULF OF MEXICO

**Stetson
Bank**

**East
Flower
Garden**

**West
Flower
Garden**

28'00 N

N

W   E

S

0   10   20 miles

93'40 W

Air Transportation

The nearest commercial aviation airports to Galveston and Freeport are **William P. Hobby Airport** (HOU, http://www.fly2houston.com/hobbyHome) and **George Bush Intercontinental Airport** (IAH, http://www.fly2houston.com/iah).

Scholes International Airport at Galveston

(GLS, www.galvestonairport.com/interior.html) is a general aviation airport with full services.

Brazoria County Airport

(LBX, www.brazoria-county.com/Airport/Index.asp) is a general aviation airport with full services within a 25-minute drive from Freeport.

Ground Transportation

Alamo, Avis, Budget, Dollar, Enterprise, Hertz, National and Thrifty rental car companies are located at **William P. Hobby Airport**.

All of the above companies, plus Advantage Car Rental, are located at **George Bush Intercontinental Airport**.

Enterprise is the only rental car company located at **Scholes International Airport at Galveston**.

Avis is the only rental car company located at **Brazoria County Airport** near Freeport.

Accommodations, Restaurants, Markets and Attractions

Because of the wide variety of commercial enterprises available to the public, we recommend that visitors check with area Chambers of Commerce for lists of local businesses in all categories, from where to stay to where to eat and what to do.

Diving Operations/Fishing Charters

In addition to accessing the Sanctuary by private boat, there are four charter (diving or fishing) boat companies which visit the three banks within the Sanctuary.

Fish-N-Divers CharterM/V Fish-N-Diver
(departs from Galveston, TX)
7 Tiki Circle Drive
Galveston, TX 77554
Telephone: 409-763-5232
Mobile: 713-304-2070
E-mail: sean@fishndivers.com
www.fishndivers.com

Fling Charters, Inc.
M/V Fling
(departs from Freeport, TX)
1203 North Avenue J
Freeport, TX 77541
Telephone: 979-233-4445
E-mail: sharon@flingcharters.com
www.flingcharters.com

Spree Expeditions, Inc.
M/V Spree
(departs from Freeport, TX)
P.O. Box 692
Muenster, TX 76252
Telephone: 281-970-0534
Toll Free: 866-460-3483
E-mail: info@spreeexpeditions.com
www.spreeexpeditions.com

True Blue Watersports
M/V Eagle Ray
(<u>departs from Galveston, TX</u>)
5959 Common Street
Lake Charles, LA 70607
Telephone: 337-310-1681
Mobile: 337-802-8529
E-mail: godive@truebluewatersports.com
www.truebluewatersports.com

Most dive professionals consider Flower Garden and Stetson Banks to be **<u>intermediate to advanced</u>** dive sites.

While conditions can be calm and suitable for beginners, those occasions are extremely rare and totally unpredictable. More typically, you will experience multiple currents, running in different directions and speeds at different depths. Currents may develop or disappear in the middle of a dive. Wave height and frequency are also quite variable and can make it difficult to re-board the boat safely. Previous saltwater experience is strongly recommended before diving in the sanctuary.

Fishing guides

See the list above in **Diving Operations/Fishing Charters**, which is a combined list of both diving and fishing operators for Flower Garden Banks.

Clean Marinas

The Clean Texas Marina Program is a partnership among the Marina Association of Texas, Texas Sea Grant College Program, Texas Commission on Environmental Quality (TCEQ) and Texas Parks & Wildlife Department (TPWD).

This program enables marinas to be recognized for their efforts in environmental responsibility. It also lets boaters identify those marinas that promote clean activities and follow best management practices. Participation is voluntary and shows a marina's commitment to keeping Texas boating areas safe and clean.

More information and a list of marinas may be found at:
www.cleanmarinas.org/certified-marinas.htm.

Remember, if you can't find what you are looking for in these pages, contact the local area Chamber of Commerce for help. Even if they don't know the answer to your question, they will find it for you. Enjoy your Sanctuary visit.

Note: If you find that our information is incorrect in any way, please send an email to publisher@oceanpublishing.org with the information you believe should be changed and we will investigate.

Céline, Fabien and Jean-Michel Cousteau. Photo credit: Carrie Vonderhaar, Ocean Futures Society.

Acknowledgments

- The *Explore the National Marine Sanctuaries with Jean-Michel Cousteau* series would not be possible without the creation of the two-hour PBS television special, *America's Underwater Treasures,* co-produced with KQED Public Broadcasting in San Francisco, the companion limited edition book *America's Underwater Treasures,* and the talented people who contributed to those projects
- Julie Robinson, co-author *America's Underwater Treasures* Limited Edition Book
- The staff at Ocean Futures Society: Charles Vinick, Sandra Squires, Lida Pardisi, Laura Brands, Carey Batha, Jim Knowlton, Brian Hall, Nathan Dembeck, Matthew Ferraro, Carrie Vonderhaar, Nancy Marr, Marie-Claude Oren
- Ocean Futures Society's Dr. Richard Murphy, Director of Science and Education; Pam Stacey, Co-Producer and writer of the film *America's Underwater Treasures*; Don Santee, Chief of Expeditions, and Holly Lohuis, Expedition Biologist for reviewing and fact checking the manuscript
- All of the members of the *America's Underwater Treasures* expedition team for sharing their stories and allowing us to explore the sanctuaries through their eyes
- Dr. Sylvia Earle for her Foreword
- Fabien and Céline Cousteau
- Dr. Jane Lubchenco, Administrator, National Oceanic and Atmospheric Administration
- Daniel Basta, Director, National Marine Sanctuary System, NOAA

- Matt Stout, Communications Director, National Oceanic and Atmospheric Administration
- Sarah Marquis, West Coast/Pacific Media Coordinator, National Marine Sanctuary System, NOAA
- Dr. Billy D. Causey, Regional Director, Southeast Atlantic, Gulf of Mexico and Caribbean Region, National Marine Sanctuaries
- National Marine Sanctuary Superintendents, especially Sean Morton (Acting Superintendent, Florida Keys), George Sedberry (Gray's Reef), G. P. Schmahl (Flower Garden Banks)
- National Marine Sanctuary Staff and Volunteers
- National Marine Sanctuary Foundation, Jason Patlis, President, and Lori Arguelles, Past-President
- Dr. Maia McGuire, Research Editor and Compiler
- Nate Myers, Cover Designs and Interior Layouts
- Mike Cavaliere – Editing and Copyediting

- And a special "Thank You" to Carrie Vonderhaar from the Ocean Publishing Team for her incredible assistance and coordination. She was absolutely terrific!

Glossary

algae: a large group of primitive plants that live mostly in water, such as kelp and other seaweeds

anemone, sea: a sea animal with a crown of tentacles at the top of a fleshy polyp or stalk, with tentacles which contain stinging cells

backreef: the area behind or to the landward side of a reef; usually includes a lagoon between the reef and the land

baleen: a tough, horny material growing in comblike fringes from the upper jaws of some species of whales; a horny keratinous substance found in two rows of transverse plates which hang down from the upper jaws of baleen whales

ballast: a heavy substance placed in such a way as to improve stability and control (as of the draft of a ship or the buoyancy of a balloon or submarine)

bedrock: the solid rock underlying unconsolidated surface materials (as soil)

benthic: on or near the bottom of a lake, river or ocean

bioaccumulate: the increase in the concentration of a substance, especially a contaminant, in an organism or in the food chain over time, as ciguatera in large grouper, mackerel and barracuda

biota: the flora and fauna of a region

coral bleaching: the process where corals under stress lose zooxanthellae living within their tissues, leaving behind the white, natural skeleton of the coral

critical habitat: defined by NOAA as: (1) specific areas within the geographical area occupied by the species at the time of listing, if they contain physical or biological features essential to conservation, and those features may require special management considerations or protection; and (2) specific areas outside the geographical area occupied by the species if the agency determines that the area itself is essential for conservation

invasive species: aquatic and terrestrial organisms and plants that have been introduced into new ecosystems throughout the United States and the world, both harming the natural resources in these ecosystems and threatening the human use of these resources

mariculture: the cultivation of marine organisms in or out of their natural environment

Marine Protected Area (MPA): defined areas where natural and/or cultural resources are given greater protection than the surrounding waters, and may span a arrange of habitats including the open oceans, coastal areas, inter-tidal zones, estuaries and the Great Lakes

no discharge zone: an area of a water body or an entire water body into which the discharge of sewage (whether treated or untreated) from vessels is completely prohibited

no-take zone: a marine protected area where catches or removal of organisms are prohibited by law

pandemics: outbreaks of a disease on a global scale

pathogens: a specific causative agent (as a bacterium or virus) of disease

pelagic: refers to animals that live in the open sea, away from the coast or seafloor

plankton blooms: a phytoplankton population explosion which occurs when sunlight and nutrients are readily available to the plants, and they grow and reproduce to a point where they are so dense that their presence changes the color of the water in which they live

polyps: an animal in the Cnidaria family which attaches to a surface and produces identical copies of itself; any sea animal with a fleshy stalk and a crown of tentacles, such as corals and sea anemones

rhizomes: a somewhat elongate usually horizontal subterranean plant stem that is often thickened by deposits of reserve food material, produces shoots above and roots below, and is distinguished from a true root in possessing buds, nodes, and usually scale-like leaves

rookeries: a breeding ground or haunt especially of gregarious birds or mammals (as penguins or seals)

Sargassum: any species of a genus (*Sargassum*) of brown algae that have a branching thallus with lateral outgrowths differentiated as leafy segments, air bladders, or spore-bearing structures

sea fan: any of various gorgonians (a soft coral species with horny and branching skeleton) with a fan-shaped skeleton

sea whip: any of various gorgonian corals with elongated flexible un-branched or little-branched whip-like colonies

sediment: the matter that settles to the bottom of a liquid

symbiosis: the living together in more or less intimate association or close union of two dissimilar organisms

watershed: a region or area bounded peripherally by a divide and draining ultimately to a particular watercourse or body of water

Wildlife Management Areas: areas set aside in many U.S. states for the conservation of wildlife and for recreational activities involving wildlife

zooplankton: planktonic organisms belonging to the animal kingdom, the majority of which are small crustaceans (copepods, krill), arrowworms, and gelatinous creatures that feed primarily on phytoplankton

zooxanthellae: tiny algae that live in the tissues of coral, which use the energy from sunlight to produce food (carbohydrates and simple amino acids)

Index

Biographies

Jean-Michel Cousteau

Explorer. Environmentalist. Educator. Film Producer. For half a century, Jean-Michel Cousteau has dedicated himself and his vast experience to communicate to people of all nations and generations his love and concern for our water planet.

Since first being "thrown overboard" by his father at the age of seven with newly invented SCUBA gear on his back, Jean-Michel has been exploring the ocean realm. The son of ocean explorer Jacques Cousteau, Jean-Michel has investigated the world's oceans aboard *Calypso* and *Alcyone* for much of his life. Honoring his heritage, Jean-Michel founded Ocean Futures Society in 1999 to carry on this pioneering work.

Ocean Futures Society, a non-profit marine conservation and education organization, serves as a "Voice for the Ocean" by communicating in all media the critical bond between people and the sea and the importance of wise environmental policy. As Ocean Future's spokesman, Jean-Michel serves as an impassioned diplomat for the environment, reaching out to the public through a variety of media.

Jean-Michel has received many awards, including the Emmy, the Peabody Award, the 7 d'Or, and the Cable Ace Award, and has produced over 80 films. Cousteau is the executive producer of the highly acclaimed PBS television *series Jean-Michel Cousteau: Ocean Adventures*. In 2006, more than three million Americans learned about the sanctuaries for the first time from the award-winning film *America's Underwater Treasures*, part of the *Ocean Adventures* series. Also in 2006, Jean-Michel's initiative to protect the Northwest Hawaiian Islands took him to The White House where he screened, *Voyage to Kure*, for President George W. Bush. The President was inspired and in June 2006, he declared the 1,200-mile chain of islands a Marine National Monument—at the time; the largest marine protected area in the world.

Jean-Michel is also one of the founders of the National Marine Sanctuary Foundation and is currently a Trustee Emeritus.

Most recently, Jean-Michel and his Ocean Futures Society team were among the first to survey and film under water at the Gulf of Mexico Deep Horizon oil spill. Their footage was used as evidence that large masses of oil and dispersant were traveling under water.

The mission of Ocean Futures Society is to explore our global ocean, inspiring and educating people throughout the world to act responsibly for its protection, documenting the critical connection between humanity and nature, and celebrating the ocean's vital importance to the survival of all life on our planet.

JEAN-MICHEL COUSTEAU'S
OCEAN
FUTURES
SOCIETY

WWW.OCEANFUTURES.ORG

"Protect the ocean and you protect yourself"

Ocean Futures Society is a non-profit 501(c)(3) organization, U.S. tax ID #95-4455199

Dr. Sylvia A. Earle

Dr. Sylvia A. Earle is a longtime friend of Jean-Michel Cousteau and has been a member of the Ocean Futures Society Advisory Board since its beginning in 1999. She is a pioneer in ocean exploration and research and is currently an Explorer-in-Residence at the National Geographic Society, leader of the Sustainable Seas Expeditions, chair of the Advisory Councils for Harte Research Institute and for the Ocean in Google Earth. Dr. Earle also served as Chief Scientist of NOAA in the early 1990s and she is a 2009 recipient of the coveted TED Prize for her proposal to establish a global network of Marine Protected Areas. Dr. Earle is one of the founders of the National Marine Sanctuary Foundation and is currently a Trustee Emeritus.

Dr. Maia McGuire

Dr. Maia McGuire, Research Editor and Compiler for this book, has been the University of Florida Sea Grant Extension Agent for northeast Florida since 2001. She holds a BS in Marine Biology and a PhD in Marine Biology and Fisheries. Prior related experience was with Harbor Branch Oceanographic Institution. Dr. McGuire is an active member in several organizations, including the National Marine Educators Association, Florida Marine Science Education Association, and the Association of Natural Resource Education Professionals, among others. She has won several honors and frequently speaks at regional and national conferences.

JMC photo: Photo credit: Carrie Vonderhaar, Ocean Futures Society
Sylvia: Photo credit: Carrie Vonderhaar, Ocean Futures Society
Maia: Photo credit: Debbi Penrose, Florida School for the Deaf and the Blind